MW01002082

HUNTED

A MEMOIR OF SURVIVAL

ROSEMARY SANGIORGIO

POWERFUL BOOKS

CONTENTS

DISCLAIMER

This is a true story of my lived experience. Names have been changed to protect individual privacy.

TRAUMA IS...

"Trauma is not what happens to you. Trauma is what happens inside you as a result of what happened to you."
Dr. Gabor Mate

PROLOGUE

CALM

There is a light salty breeze dancing in the courtyard to help tolerate the summer heat. My hair is still wet from showering after the beach, which ordinarily helps keep me cooler but today there seems to be no escape. There are fires in the mountains nearby and the breeze coming from the hills is warm too. The only way to deal with the heat is patience and a mindful affinity to the shade.

I am four years old and in the Calabrian seaside town where my mother was raised, visiting my grandparents for the summer. Some of my aunts, uncles and cousins have also arrived from the US to visit, but it seems everyone has scurried away after lunch to rest. My mother is nowhere to be seen and I am hoping she is going to forget all about my afternoon nap. I spot a small lizard that has come out of hiding from behind my grandmother's plants, climbing up the wall in energetic bursts. I observe the little creature rising quickly and then freezing every few feet to survey the territory until gradually vanishing from sight. My eyes shift to the edges of the tablecloth swaying in the wind. The sunlight cuts through the cloth making it look like a wedding veil if not for the grandiose orange and brown floral design imprinted on the material.

"Rosa! Can you check the table for anything left to wash?" My grandmother breaks me out of my reverie, and I respond, "No, Nonna, there is nothing left."

My grandfather is sitting at the head of the table with a cutting board in front of him. He's enjoying his usual post-meal cheese plate while sipping wine in the sun. His dark, waxy fisherman's hands are clean but weathered from working at sea. That morning I had heard my grandfather's boats come in and I had jumped out of bed to collect the dead or dying seahorses and starfish caught in the nets.

It is quiet except for the running water and clinking cutlery. Pretty soon I'm sure my mother will find me and shoo me off, but for now I will stay leaning against the doorway facing the courtyard and watching my grandfather eat cheese until she figures out where I am.

My grandfather looks at me and catches my stare. He smiles and asks, "Did you want some?" I look at him and respond, "No, thank you." He chuckles while taking another piece of cheese from his plate and looks at it for a moment before lifting his head towards the sky and holding it above his mouth. As he holds the morsel in the air, I clearly see what everyone was discussing at lunch was true. Suspended there, but hanging onto the cheese for dear life, were small white worms. He dropped the piece into his mouth. "Are you sure?" he asked while chewing. "Yes, I'm sure, Nonno, thank you," I respond, somehow remembering my manners while still in shock of what I had just witnessed. My grandfather had come home for lunch that day excited that he had found some 'casu martzu' at the market. I didn't believe everyone at the table when I heard them chatter about how the cheese had worms in it and how it is eaten with the live worms inside, so I had to see for myself.

I watch him eat in fascinated disgust, while taking sips of wine and bites of bread until I hear my mother call out, "Rosa! Where are you? It's time for sleep!' I turn towards her voice slightly relieved by her interruption. She walks into the kitchen and takes me by the hand and then laughs when she realizes I'm watching her father eat the wormy cheese.

I let her lead me into the room where we slept, and I climb into bed to lay down. She sits beside me using the wall as a backrest while flipping through her crosswords to find the latest one she was working on. I am tired at this point and feel warm and safe in the presence of my mother. I didn't want to fall asleep, but it is a losing battle between my fatigue and my desire to stay awake. The faint smell of her perfume is in the room, and I eventually doze off watching her thinking over the crossword puzzle she is working on. I feel safe in her presence and know inherently that I am loved and cherished. I trust her and feel she is strong and beautiful. There was no one in the world that knows me better than my mother and I am grateful for her. Her love is like a soft cocoon around me protecting me from harm, but still giving me enough room to be myself. I sleep deeply and peacefully knowing I have nothing or no one to fear.

Open Season

I race out of the room quickly and in a bit of a daze. It is late at night and all the lights are off in the house except for the glow of the TV behind me. I am scared and confused and speed silently up the stairs two at a time. I don't understand what just happened. *Why did Lyle just do that to me? Why did he touch me like that? Did he forget who I was?*

I had gotten up from bed that night to watch Saturday Night Live in the living room. I did this regularly on the weekends without telling anyone and felt like it was my own secret adventure. At twelve years old, these were the type of things I would think of as adventures.

Depending on the show's roster each week, I would wait 'til the house was quiet and then tiptoe downstairs into the living room to watch it. I was always mindful going down the stairs and avoided the creaky top step so that no one would hear me. That weekend was no different and as I sat there watching the door opened and Lyle, my cousin Tamara's husband, walked in. I had met him years earlier when I stood as a flower girl for his wedding to Tamara. As soon as he entered the room alone I felt awkward. *Is he here to tell me to stop watching TV and go to bed?* I thought. I knew if my parents caught me in the den they'd tell me to go right to sleep. He made small talk and asked what I was watching before closing the door and sitting down on the couch next to me. I was not excited about his company, but did not want to be rude and leave the room either. *Why is he here?* I kept thinking. I liked him and thought he was nice enough, but I wanted to be alone and didn't understand why he wasn't upstairs in bed sleeping. Tamara and Lyle arrived from the US to visit my family, however it was the end of their vacation, and they were leaving the next day. I would not see them since I was going skiing with my brother and heading out early in the morning. We had all spent time together in the kitchen after dinner exchanging our goodbyes and promises to see one another as soon as we could. *Why was he here then?* I kept thinking.

Once the show was over, I got up from the couch to head to bed. "Good night," I said as I made my way out of the room. "Wait. Aren't you going to say good-bye?" Lyle asked. I turn to see him getting up from the couch. "Sure of course." I respond slightly confused since I already had said goodbye. He stands with arms outstretched, and knees slightly bent so that I can reach up to him and give him a hug. After a few seconds I begin to let go but instead of Lyle doing the same thing, he pulls me tighter towards him. I stand there wondering what is happening when I suddenly feel his hands on my tiny breasts groping them. I stand there motionless feeling his hands on me. My body is frozen. *WHAT IS HE DOING!* I scream inside. *WHY IS HE TOUCHING ME LIKE THAT? WHAT IS HAPPENING? HE IS NOT SUPPOSED TO BE DOING THIS. WHY IS HE DOING THIS? WHAT IS HAPPENING? WHAT IS HAPPENING?* I feel like screaming but I can't do a thing. I feel paralyzed. *WHY CAN'T I MOVE! MOVE! MOVE! MOVE!* I repeat to myself until I am able to push back but whimper as I can't get out of his grasp. He is holding my body hostage while his hands grope and touch me all over. I am trapped and I am terrified. He is breathing hard while holding me close and through his breathing I hear him whisper *"It's okay."* I don't know if he is talking to me or himself while I am trying to escape. He continues to grope me, switching arms and hands so that he maintains control of my body. I wriggle and continue pushing back until I am out of his arms. I dash out of the room and climb the stairs quickly closing my bedroom door silently behind me. I turn and crawl over my bed and make it to the corner of the room where I hide between the wall and my night-stand. I sit and wait but hear no sounds telling me I had been followed. I sit still, waiting. After a few minutes I hear him slowly walking up the stairs and listen carefully to count the steps he takes. *Where is he? Is he coming in here? Please don't let him come in here.* The closer he gets, the more my body tries to retreat into itself. I hear the creak of the top step and hold my breath. He is a few feet from my bedroom door, and he is not moving. I am shaking, barely breathing, trying to hear *anything* but I hear nothing. I don't know where he is anymore. I knew he reached the top of the stairs, but I can't figure out where he is. I stare at the doorknob of my room and wait. *What is he doing? Why isn't he going into his room?* Finally, I hear him take a step and open the door to the bedroom where he is staying with my cousin, and the squeak of the mattress as his body eases into it. I relax slightly and try to catch my racing thoughts in an attempt to understand what happened but could not make sense of any of it. *Why did he do that to me? What was he doing? Does he even know what he did?* I climb into bed quietly and curl into a little ball. I am too scared to sleep and too tired to stay awake. I sleep intermittently and wake before the sun comes up. As soon as I open my eyes I sit up quickly remembering the night before and scan the room to check if he is there. My door is closed and everything in the room is how I remember. Nothing has been moved or shifted. He is not here. I take a deep breath and relax falling back into my pillows. The house is still quiet, and I know my brother will be tapping on my door soon to head out. In the meantime, I do not feel safe enough to venture out to the bathroom to freshen up. *What if he is there?* I think fearfully. *I don't want him touching me again.* I hear a toilet flush in my parents' bathroom but after a few minutes I realize whoever got up went back to bed. I take a breath and exhale settling further into my pillows to watch the sun come up in my room. My stomach is bothering me but I'm sure I'll feel better once I eat something. After a few minutes I can't stand the feeling in my stomach, so I reach over to my nightstand and pick up a book. *That's better,* I think. *I'll read until Philip comes to get me.* I didn't want to think of the night before because every time I did, I felt sick.

ONE
LA FAMIGLIA

I was twelve years old the first time he touched me and twelve years old when my life changed. There has always been a before and after. If I remember my early childhood before the abuse, I generally felt happy and safe. I can recall my dad playing Santa Claus for Christmas and coming into the house with a big bag of presents for my cousins, brothers and me. I remember seeing him walk in and being stunned that 'Santa' had come to our house. I had no idea it was my dad and when my father returned to the party out of costume, I raced over excited to tell him about the special visit. I remember jumping into my dad's arms feeling a tinge of sadness that he had missed such a monumental event.

I was Daddy's girl when I was little and would only respond to him calling me princess and he would get a kick out of calling me princess after he realized I wouldn't respond to any other word. Many nights he would come home after I went to bed and when I would hear him I'd sneak out of my room to run down the hall and tackle him with a hug. He would always pick me up and hug me tight right back. His hugs were warm and enveloping and made me feel safe and special. Mornings were my favourite because of how he used to wake me up to get ready for school. He would gently touch my hair to wake me up and whisper in my ear "Rosaaa, time to get up," and I'd wake up gently, without any feeling of unease. Most of the time I'd get a nice little back rub too while he coaxed me to wake up urging me to use the bathroom before my brothers woke up and took over the house. My dad did all sorts of special things for me, and I knew it. He bought me KitKat's all the time and asked me to share with my brothers. I said it was hard because of they were four bars, and we were three siblings. From then on he brought two home so there would be one for me, and one for my brothers to share. He knew it was not fair, but he let it slide. Once in a while he'd bring three home, just to mix it up. My dad whistled a lot around the house and when I learned to whistle too, he and I would whistle back and forth to each other. It was a little game we liked to play. Sometimes, he'd come home to what he'd think was an empty house and I would be by the fireplace reading. He would whistle when he walked through the door, and I'd respond so he knew someone was home.

When I was a little girl I would play outside in the front and backyard of my childhood home lifting garden stones to watch the insects beneath scurry from the light. I would create terrariums in old mason jars complete with bugs and foliage using a screwdriver to hammer air holes into the lids. I would keep the jars in the garage for a few days for observational purposes, and then gently empty them back out into the garden as soon as my curiosities were satisfied and my notes complete. Science and nature fascinated me and for a while I wanted to become a veterinarian. If I wasn't outside exploring I spent days playing 'house' with my mom and would bring her imaginary tea and cookies from the downstairs playroom while my husband was "at work". I spent a lot of time with my mom in the kitchen watching her cook, but I preferred baking. On the days she would cook for dinner guests, I would help her with the prep and usually make Crème Caramel for dessert. I perfected the recipe she taught me, and everyone would marvel at how good it tasted and be shocked when my mother would tell them I made it. My mom would never tell guests I had made the dessert but would smile proudly at me once the compliment arose and I was asked to explain it.

I was a slightly anxious child, but overall loved speaking with people and uncovering my world. I would become a chatterbox once I was comfortable with someone and was frequently punished at school for talking too much during class. Detentions were not uncommon for me, but they didn't help my behaviour. Even when one of my teachers placed my desk right beside his after Christmas break until the end of the scholastic year, it would not discourage me from speaking with my classmates.

Reading and the world of the written word was my passion. I was a voracious bookworm and devoured every book in sight. My parents could barely keep up with my hobby so I satiated myself by finding books to read whenever and wherever I could. I ordered books from the book club at school and while other students purchased one or two books, I used to receive a box of books for myself. Libraries were my haven and each week when our classroom would visit the school library for story time, I would sit in the front row and listen attentively to the librarian as she used different voices for the characters. After story time we would be permitted to borrow one book with our library cards. The books I would choose were more advanced than the grade I was in but nonetheless, I would finish the book I borrowed within a few days and then wait, what seemed like forever, to borrow another one. I began asking friends if I could use their library cards to get more books and once the librarian caught onto what I was doing she kept her eye on me and eventually gave me a job. The librarian gave me free access to the library whenever I wanted and in return, I helped other children in my school learn how to spell and read.

I wrote my first book at ten years old and from then on I adored spending time at the local library discovering new authors, reading poetry or copying my favourite poems and passages in notebooks to bring home with me. Seeing words on a page or being in the presence of books made me feel calm and centered. I felt words. Symbols would emboss the pages I read, entering my consciousness creating a stream of pictures and emotions. Reading was like having a magic wand that would whisk me away into any world I wanted to see. My childhood was sheltered, and books gave me an escape to understand and marvel at wonders that I was still too young to experience. Travelling for the summer to my grandparents' home in Italy always required me sneaking the biggest and thickest paperbacks I could into the suit-cases of family members, so I had enough to read over the summer. I always ran out of course, but once I learned how to read Italian, I would buy books and comics in Italian while on vacation.

My parents were much more lenient with me during the summers in Italy. I couldn't wait to get there so that I could run feral on the beach every day playing with my cousins and jumping off my grandfathers' anchored fishing boats. My maternal grandfather was poor when he was young, however over the years managed to establish a very successful fishing and seafood distribution company with his brothers. My grandfather used his wealth to purchase a house in town and, years later renovated it to add an apartment for each of his five children so that they would have a place to stay when they came to visit. The building still stands and is where my grandparents' children and grandchildren continue to summer at their leisure. The original house was built under the fascist government of Mussolini and was designated for the medical doctor in town. Once the doctor retired, my grandfather bought the house and lived there until his children moved on with families of their own. I remember the renovations very well since for a little while, after the structure was built, my cousins and I used to play in the concrete and brick wall rooms during the day. Down on the beach, men would skeet shoot near the fishing freezers, and I recall us having access to an incredible amount of empty shotgun shells that we turned into toys and mobiles with my grandfather's fishing lines and other odds and ends we'd find in the house and on the fishing boats.

My grandparents were from the same little town in Calabria and met when my grandmother Rose moved across the street from him. My grandmother's siblings were not close to her in age, so they married and moved out of the house while she was still young. My grandmother on the other hand, had a lot to learn before becoming betrothed herself so she spent her days mastering household chores like cleaning, cooking, sewing, needle-working and preserving food. Besides developing life skills and going to school, my grandmother also learned about family dynamics, morals, and values by regularly attending mass and being a devout Catholic. During his papacy from 1878 to 1903, Pope Leo published several encyclicals that were distributed to Roman Catholic bishops to clarify the official teachings of the Catholic faith. Pope Leo was known for being "modern" as he worked tirelessly to reconcile Catholic ideologies in a corrupted misogynistic social landscape.

---

11. The woman, because she is flesh of his flesh, and bone of his bone, must be subject to her husband and obey him; not, indeed, as a servant, but as a companion, so that her obedience shall be wanting in neither honor nor dignity. Since the husband represents Christ, and since the wife represents the Church, let there always be, both in him who commands and in her who obeys, a heaven-born love guiding both in their respective duties."

ITEM 11 & 12. ARCANUM ENCYCLICAL
OF POPE LEO XIII

My grandmother's marriage to my grandfather not only gave her the opportunity to have and raise children, but also gave her family an opportunity to become an integral part of the patron saint festival that takes place in August each year. Organizers would use my grandfather's fishing boats to carry the statue of Mother Mary as well as the clergy and choir in a seaside procession. At the time of my grandmother's death, she didn't remember much, but she did remember the prayers and hymns she learnt in church and would recite them with you if you began to say them out loud. I remember my grandmother Rose as a warm woman that smiled often. Her eyes were hazel but more on the greenish side and her skin felt like satin. When she laughed her eyes squinted and became smaller yet wouldn't close. I remember her always smiling except when we would go back home to Canada. There was a lot of sadness when the summers came to an end, and it felt awful to see my mother in such a desperate state each time she left her family. In the car on the way to the airport I would reach for my mother's hand to hold and comfort her, but if she was overwhelmed with grief, she wouldn't take it. If she didn't hold my hand I would rest it on the seat between us so that she could reach out for comfort if needed. After a little while I would always feel her reach out to me and hold my hand. I would sit still knowing not to look into her eyes as that would instigate more tears. We would sit in silence for the hour-long drive to the airport and by the time we got there my mother was on autopilot. She knew exactly what to do and didn't speak much until a few days after returning home.

My grandmother was strict with her children because of her upbringing, but also because my grandfather was not always present as his work would take him away for days or weeks at a time. She had other women that helped her with taking care of the home and children while my grandfather was away, but she did not like being alone.

My grandmother had five children and three that ended up marrying and living nearby. Her other two daughters were in the US and Canada. Each year my grandmother would be visited by her children and grandchildren from far away and make lunch for about fifteen to twenty people in the stifling hot summer while we were all at the beach. I never heard her complain once though. She missed her children that lived far away and did whatever she did with a smile and a hug. Each day after my nap I would walk down to the corner store to get a single serve ice-cream treat. The freezer was big, and the shop lady had to help with retrieving my desired item. She was a tiny woman with a wonderfully friendly face and eyes that seemed to sparkle when she spoke to you. The shop lady had a small step stool set nearby enabling her to reach down into the freezer and grab an item. Once I chose, she would tell me to come back and pay another time, yet I never paid, not even once. I found out after my grandmother passed that there was a running tab for my ice cream addiction in which my grandmother squared up weekly on my behalf.

My mother Eva was born in June 1946 which was the same year that 89% of Italians voted in a referendum to abolish the monarchy and form a republic. The referendum was the first-time women were permitted to vote in Italy and in the years following, northern Italy saw a boom in economy and quality of life. Unfortunately, southern Italy did not have the same experience and the destruction of the war did not give rise to reparation in the south. Families struggled to make ends meet well into the late 50's but my mother's family did not. The fishing business that my grandfather had built with his brothers was a lucrative one that enabled my grandfather to buy a fair amount of property in town as well as enjoy small luxuries like an indoor bathroom and television set in his home. Sometimes, he would perch the TV on the windowsill facing the street for soccer games, new films or news so that neighbors were able to watch as well.

My mother and her sisters did not have a very active social life and the friends and acquaintances they did have were usually family members or people living nearby. They lived and operated within the radius of their home, the beach in front of their home, school, or the church down the street. Besides that, they were not permitted to venture out or go out with friends unless they were with their brothers or parents.

My father Gabriel's childhood was quite different from my mother's as he grew up on a small family estate farm in the hills of the next coastal town to the south. My father was born in 1942 and lived on the farm until he was fourteen years old. Post-war Italy was hard on him and his family, so he left for Canada and travelled across the Atlantic for two weeks on an ocean liner. My dad landed in Halifax and then headed to Toronto to meet other immigrants that had already made the trip. He moved into a home on Symington Avenue and straightaway began school to learn a trade opening his first hair salon at eighteen years old. Once the salon was established, my dad began attending conferences, trade shows and competitions to create a name for himself in the industry. In the 1960's my father was a competitive platform hair artist that travelled the US and Canada competing with others in his line of work. His accomplishments were noticed and soon the salon was a busy and bustling business. By the time my dad was in his early 20's the salon was doing well, and he was able to afford a ticket back home to visit family and friends.

My father's family knew my mother's family however my parents did not meet until later when my dad returned to Italy for a visit. They met at a dance on the beach and my dad showed up at my mother's door a few days later to speak with my grandfather and ask his permission to become acquainted with his daughter. My grandfather accepted the proposition once my mother confirmed that she would also like to know my father. My mom's brother on the other hand, warned her of moving forward with the relationship as he knew his sister did not want to leave Italy. In the end, my mother chose my father despite knowing his ties to Canada. Although it was not an arranged marriage in the sense that my mother was required to marry him, both sets of parents roughly set them up to meet and paved the way once my mother accepted my father's advancement. They eventually dated with all the appropriate permissions, logistics and chaperones in place, and in due course my dad asked my grandfather whether he could marry his daughter. My grandfather accepted and so did my mother on the condition that they would move back to Italy after a few years in Canada. My father loosely agreed, and they married in August of 1968.

My parents' relationship was a rocky one and I remember a lot of fighting, tears, and tension behind the veil of perfection that was displayed to the world. I remember the fighting between my parents happening much more often after we moved from the house from where my brothers Philip, Joseph and I were born, to a bigger house where we each had our own rooms and an enormous backyard. I buried myself in reading to tune out my parents but when the arguing became physical, my nervous system did not take well to the ever-constant underlying apprehension. I was constantly on edge and fearing my father would hurt my mother in a fit of rage. The arguments were always about money despite my father's successful business and extravagant generosity, but only for what he felt was important. My mother did not have her own bank account and was forced to ask for money for anything that was needed in the home. For some reason, each time she did, my father would become upset even though she never bought anything more than groceries or gas. Some days it was a small argument, but other days were much worse. I will never forget the day I heard them arguing and listening to my mother screaming and fighting my dad off her as my brother raced down the stairs to stop them. I stood at the top of the staircase clutching both handrails screaming incoherently after my mother raced past me up the stairs to get away. My dad followed after her but had to pry my hands off the railings to do so. Once he did I used my free arms and hands to attach myself to my father thinking I could somehow stop the argument. He picked me up and I thought it was over but to my horror, my dad began making his way over to where my mother was. I began screaming louder and louder the closer he got to her as I was terrified he was going to harm her with me in his arms. He attempted to put me down, but I would not let him as I was crying uncontrollably, whimpering and pleading for him to stop. He eventually lowered his voice and after a few minutes put me down to say something to my mother, but she was weeping and would not respond. I remember my father turned to look at me and my brother, and then walked past us out of the room, and out of the front door. We heard the car start up and drive away while my brother and I watched in silence as my mother took some time to pull herself together. I don't know how she did it, but she did it. The fight was one of many, not all physical; yet even if they weren't physical, they left my brothers and I shaking the entire time, waiting to jump up and save her. Eventually my mother began working for herself and building a little business of her own selling high quality household linens like bedding and bath sets. She would have an open house and invite ladies to our home or go to their home to sell or order product. It was a lot of work and a lot of driving so she eventually switched to a steady retail job instead. Once she started making money and getting out of the house, my parents relationship changed, however they never really got along.

I did not learn much from my parents' relationship except that I didn't want to have the same kind when I grew up. Although I was Daddy's girl when I was a small child, I changed my tune after watching my mother weaken or submit and nonetheless continue to have difficulties with my father. I became very protective of her and defended her against him when and if I could. Seeing her cry or upset would break my heart and ignite rage in me. I didn't hate him, but it was hard for me to love him. His behavior towards my mother was ignored and heavily misunderstood by his own family and my mother felt very alone with her struggles. Her escape was travelling to Italy in the summer, and spending time in the US with her sister in the winter. Her sister Bianca was older than her and my mother looked up to her like a mother figure. That sentiment, coupled with the fact that they were on the same continent and could more easily relate to one another's experiences created a strong bond between them.

TWO

SPILLING THE BEANS

I was seventeen when I let my mother know what my cousin's husband was doing to me. I hadn't told anyone before her except for a classmate when I was thirteen years old. He let me know I should speak with my parents about it and that what Lyle was doing was called sexual abuse. "Even though he didn't rape me?" I asked. "Yes," my friend confirmed. "That happened to my mother, which is why I know what I'm talking about." My mind stopped. "Your mother?" I asked. "Ya. With my grandfather. Something happened between them when she was young, and he didn't rape her either. You need to tell your parents. No one should be touching you the way he did."

The words *sexual abuse* frightened me. It was the first time I had said something out loud about what was happening to me and the first time I heard those words attached to Lyle's behaviour. I knew what he was doing was wrong but did not classify it as sexual abuse since we hadn't had sexual intercourse. Quite frankly, my mind did not classify it at all. I avoided thinking about the abuse entirely and pushed it out of my mind each time it happened. Once I had the conversation with my friend, I felt ashamed and angry and much more frightened as I had no idea how to stop it from happening. Although we lived in different countries, I was spending time with these family members a few times a year for weeks at a time either at my family home in Canada, their home in Florida or the beach house in Italy. My parents never travelled for leisure, they travelled to see family, which meant I did too. I was raised to love and accept family unconditionally and although I understood that he was not a blood relative, in my mind he was family. The summer I turned seventeen was by far the worst in relation to the abuse I endured. He had already been abusing me for four years, and each time he did, it was something more blatant and forward than the last. I would never know what to expect and it was as though he followed me. Someway and somehow, he would find a way to be alone with me. By the end of that summer, I came home trembling and did so on and off for about two years after that.

I wake up in the middle of the night to see him standing in the semi-darkness of the doorway. I freeze and close my eyes slowly, hoping like hell he didn't notice that I had woken up. I lay there with my eyes closed barely breathing and playing 'dead' to the best of my ability. My body is frozen, and I am absolutely terrified of what will happen next. I feel my entire body on high alert. I have no idea what he is doing and why he is in the doorway. I open my eyes slightly so that I can see through my lashes. He is still standing there motionless and staring at me. After a few minutes he leaves, goes to the bathroom and I hear the toilet flush. I wait to hear what he does next but when he comes out of the bathroom, he walks back into the room he is sharing with my cousin and closes the door. I don't sleep for the rest of the night and lie awake until I hear the sounds of people waking up and the smell of freshly made espresso wafting into my room.

I wake up again in the middle of the night and see his silhouette in the dark sitting at the foot of my bed. Instantly my body responds, and a rush of adrenaline floods my bloodstream preparing my body to fight or flee. My muscles contract and my stomach drops almost causing me to urinate. The tension I use to keep my urine from escaping my body causes a wave of nausea but no matter how hard I try, I cannot move. I feel my insides rushing as though a dam failed somewhere within the confines of my body, yet I can't get out of the wave of the water that is rushing over me and holding me down and in place. I lay there, frozen in fear and hoping like hell my bladder will not let me down. All of this happens in a matter of seconds. As I pretend to sleep I mercilessly scold and insult myself in my mind for not finding a functional key to the room so that I'd be able to lock the door. I had looked all over the beach house and borrowed keys from other doors to see if they would work on my bedroom door. Unfortunately, none of the keys worked and here I was again completely frozen in fear.

"Okay," I tell myself "Let it happen. He will leave you alone once he gets what he wants." I exhale slowly and continue to curse my body for not reacting the way I want it to. My mind is racing and I'm trying to send messages to my limbs to jump up and run, but instead I lay there, frozen and hating my body more and more with each passing second for not doing what I want it to. Suddenly his breathing changes and I feel the bed moving rhythmically. Another wave of

nausea washes over me as I realize what he is doing. The bed finally stops moving and he stands up and walks out of the room. My eyes are closed, and I keep them closed until I hear him go into the bathroom and close the door. I feel ashamed, defeated and brutally blame myself for his behavior since I didn't stop it. I open my eyes in the dark and wonder if he will be making another visit. A few minutes later I hear him open the bathroom door and walk in the opposite direction of my room. I lay awake the rest of the night staring blankly at shadows as they move across the walls. All I wanted to do was disappear. I couldn't handle it anymore. I just never knew when or where he was going to catch me next time, because there was always a next time.

I am at the beach under an umbrella and completely immersed in a book. I am not paying attention to anything but the pages in front of me. Suddenly out of nowhere I hear, "Can I touch your bikini line?" I look up and there he is, sitting in the shade of another nearby umbrella, staring at my crotch area. I look around quickly to see who is around. As usual, no one is within earshot. I start to shake and my eyes dart towards a familiar voice. My mother is chatting with friends, and I see his wife taking a swim. I get up quickly and collect my things to leave. As I do, he continues to comment "Where are you going? I just want to feel how smooth it is. It amazes me how your bikini line can be so smooth and your skin so beautiful. Usually when it's shaved there it's bumpy, but your skin isn't. Please, can you let me feel it? It's not a big deal. I just want to touch you there."

I look at him and he's not looking at me while he's speaking. Instead he is looking around the beach to ensure no one can hear him. I leave and go home to shower and be alone until lunchtime where I know I will see him again, stuffing the hole in his face with food. The mere thought of seeing him again made me sick.

I am outside reading on the balcony. It is afternoon and everyone is asleep. Birds are chirping and it will be another half hour until the house starts to wake up. Behind me I hear a noise and suddenly Lyle's voice behind me saying, "Maybe one day soon you'll let me take photos of you in the nude. Do you think you'd let me do that?" I jump up and leave the balcony immediately while hearing him talk as I walk away. I find an empty bathroom and lock myself in. I sit there listening to the other side of the door and after a few minutes, I settle into the empty tub to read and wait until I hear the house bustle awake again.

I am sleeping on the couch and wake to feel and see his body leaning into me. He is standing and using one of his hands on the backrest of the couch to steady himself while he continues to lower his body onto mine. As I feel him coming closer I open my eyes and this time instead of freezing, I put my hands in front of my chest and push him hard. "What the fuck are you doing?" I hiss. He pulls back and stands up to look at me. "I just wanted to say good-bye," he says. He looks at me smirking and then starts to chuckle. I do not break eye contact with him and remain silent. He starts to laugh at me and walks out of the room. Why doesn't he leave me alone? What is wrong with him? I think. I feel satisfaction that this time my body 'worked' and did what I told it to. For a moment, I am strong, and I have won.

· · ·

It is scorching hot and the first day of my period. I'm feeling awful in the summer heat and am home from the beach reading in the coolness of my mother's bedroom with a fan pointed in my direction. Everyone in the house has gone to the beach and in an hour or so I was to set up the table for lunch. I was on the terrace when everyone left and grateful for having spotted Lyle in the group as well. I went downstairs to make myself a snack completely relaxed since I knew there was no one lurking about. As I stood there making a sandwich slightly leaning against the kitchen counter, I hear a shuffle behind me. Before I register the sound, I feel Lyle's body behind me and against mine. I freeze as I feel his hands travel along my body touching and groping me while licking and kissing my neck. I can feel his arousal against my body and am even more petrified when I realize he has me trapped. He continues to assault me while I remain frozen in fear. Quickly he begins to change his position with one hand on my breast and one hand on my back pushing down to lower my head towards the kitchen counter. Is this it? I think. Is this how I'm going to lose my virginity? I see the countertop getting closer and I squeeze my eyes shut.

Somehow my body comes back online and so I twist out of his grasp, run out of the apartment, and dash up the stairs into my mother's bathroom. I lock myself in and sit in front of the door with my hand on the key, making sure I expose a line of vision through the keyhole. I am crying but annoyed with the tears since they cause my vision to become blurred. I hurriedly brush them away so that I can see through the keyhole. I sit there staring through the keyhole until I feel the coast is clear and then I get up and grab a towel from the counter. I return to the door and turn the key to a vertical position and place the towel over the door handle so that there would be no way someone (he) could peek through. I turn the taps on in the bathtub and let myself cry as I undress with my back towards the mirror. I can't stand to look at myself. I step into the tub and sit down giving into my tears and shaking body until I can shower and put on a face to pretend nothing is wrong. I wash my body scrubbing hard where he was and where I could reach using a large wash-cloth to reach my back.

We had gotten back from vacationing in Italy a few weeks earlier and my parents were arguing in the kitchen about something or other. I was waiting for the right time to tell them what was going on, but since we'd got back my parents spent every moment together arguing. It was exhausting hearing them fight all the time, trying to find an opportunity where my mother wasn't upset, or my dad wasn't in a bad mood. I sat on the living room couch hearing them yet again and seeing no end in sight to their madness. As the volume between them increased I decide to call my mother into the room to let her know what was going on. I understood at that point that if I didn't say anything, it would just be a matter of time before the inevitable happened. At the very least maybe this could stop their fighting and they can focus on something else.

"MOM!" I call out. A few seconds later my mom opens the door, clearly at her wits end with my father, "Yes. What do you want?" she asks quickly. "I need to tell you something," I respond, "and if you and dad would spend a little less time fighting you would see that we have bigger problems in this family." She stops and looks at me confused, "What do you mean?" she asks. "I mean," I respond, "that someone in this family is doing something bad to me and has been doing it for a long time." My mother steps into the room and closes the door. "Who? What are you talking about?" she asks while walking over to the couch to sit next to me. I realize this is the moment I will tell her and become overwhelmed with thoughts of what might happen to my family and to him when I tell my mother the truth.

I start to cry as I tell her someone in the family has been sexually abusing me for four years and that the first time it happened, I was twelve years old. She stared at me without a word and did not interrupt. Initially, I could barely utter his name. I was frightened and ashamed of the words that were coming out of my mouth in front of my mother. She never had 'the talk' with me so any vocabulary that I was using to express what had happened was unfamiliar territory. There was so much I could not tell her because I was embarrassed and felt that it was somehow my fault or that I allowed it to happen. I didn't understand that the way I froze whenever he did something was because my body's fight or flight response reacting to the abuse. I told her the story of what happened four years earlier in that very same living room the first time he touched me and told her of a few things that had happened over that summer. We didn't speak for very long, but I was satisfied with the information I shared with her and thought she understood I had been sexually abused by my cousin's husband. My mother listened intently and when I was done speaking, she told me we would talk about this again soon. She didn't say much to me and for the first time, I could not read my mother's reaction or feeling. I knew she was not mad at me, but that was about it. She seemed distracted. She left the room and returned to the kitchen where her and my father continued to argue. I sat in the living room wondering what would happen next and hoping I wouldn't have to tell my father any of the things I told my mother. I figured she would tell him and was relieved that I had finally said something. For the first time in a while, I felt powerful.

The next day my mother woke me up to let me know I was not going to school. "I made an appointment with the psychiatrist so that we can talk about what you told me last night." I did not see the need for a discussion with him but did what my mother asked as she was obviously shaken by the conversation and didn't know how to move forward. Neither did I. My mother had been seeing a psychiatrist for a nervous cough, so she was able to set an appointment quickly.

We left for the doctor later that day and drove in silence. My mother went into the room first and I sat in the waiting room for a little while before I was called in. I was a bit more relaxed after telling my mother about the abuse so I waited hopefully and patiently knowing that I was safe and that I would finally receive some help. I walked into the office and sat down in the chair in front of him. He asked me to tell him what happened, and I told him what I had told my mother.

"Did you have sexual intercourse with him?" he asked. "No," I responded feeling ashamed that I was so wounded by Lyle's behaviour, nonetheless. "He didn't do that, but he tried to over the summer." I added, feeling his hand on my back again as though he was right behind me. I could feel my hands beginning to tremble but clasped them and fidgeted with them hoping no one would notice. *Why am I feeling his hand on my back? He's not here. What is happening?* I start to feel sick to my stomach and ask the doctor if I can leave the room to use the bathroom. I leave and run to the washroom to wet my face. *What the hell is going on? Why did I feel his hand on my back?* I stare at my reflection and take a deep breath to calm myself before heading back into the waiting room. The door to the office is closed. I wait for a while until my mother opens the door and lets me know we were heading home. Nothing more was discussed that day or the days following. I stayed in my room mostly reading books and wondering what was going to happen next.

About a week or so later my mother let me know we were leaving for Florida in a few days.

"Why are we going?" I asked.

"We are going so that we can speak with Lyle and for you to say what you want to him. Don't worry. We will be in the room with you," my mother replied. *But I didn't want to confront him,* I think, *I'm scared of him.* I didn't understand the point of this. Why wasn't anyone calling the police? The last thing I wanted was to be in a room with him. I started panicking and could feel my throat constricting. *I can't be near him! I don't want to be near him! Why is this happening?* I think. *Why doesn't she understand?*

"We are putting him on trial," my mother explained. "The family is putting him on trial." I didn't understand what this meant, and she didn't provide a clear answer or one that made sense to me. He needed to be arrested and charged, but when I brought that up, my mother responded that this was the best course of action. "What if someone doesn't believe you?" she asked me, "Or what if someone blamed you for what happened?" I quickly understood that trying to convince my mother to call the police was like talking to a brick wall. She completely shut down any scenario's having to do with bringing him to proper lawful justice. How could she do this to me after I told her what he did? Does she not understand how afraid of him I am and that it doesn't matter who is around? I talk about all of these things, yet her reassurances do not make me feel settled. I do not want to go to Florida and speak to Lyle within the confines of a ridiculous situation that would ultimately solve nothing, however I did what I was told as I had no choice.

"What am I supposed to say?" I ask still raging inside. My mother and I are in Florida sitting in my cousin Regina's room. I am aware of other family members in the house including my cousin Tamara, her sister, Regina, and my Aunt and Uncle. Lyle had not yet arrived when we were all ushered into different rooms by my mother and her sister once we knew he was on his way. "Say whatever you want," my mother responds. "Tell him what you told me that night." I was dumbfounded, still reeling in shock that I needed to be in the same room with him again. I knew I was safe, but it didn't matter. I was petrified of my predator and felt small and weak. The last time I was in a room with him he tried to rape me. *How did this get so complicated?* I thought. I had been instructed never to discuss what Lyle did to me with my cousin Tamara and now I was being told I could say whatever I wanted to Lyle. Why am I being forced to talk with him? There is nothing to smooth over or decide upon. Lyle sexually abused me so the only thing I didn't understand was everyone's calmness about the entire situation. *The issue was big. There was a crime committed. What the fuck was the point to all of this?* I thought. *Is he going to be arrested?* I snap back to reality when I hear my mother say, "Your father will be in the room so you can say whatever you want." "What do you mean my father will be in the room?" I ask.

"You will be in the living room with Dad, Lyle and Regina," my mother responds. "What about you?" I ask.

"I won't be there, but don't worry, your dad will be

there," my mother responds. *Don't worry.* I thought. My heart sank. This wasn't going to work. Whatever they were doing or trying to do made no sense. I could never express what Lyle had done to me while my father was in the room. I could barely tell my mother and was now expected to have the same type of conversation with my father and perpetrator in the room. *And why was I the only one at this bullshit trial speaking up?* I thought. Shouldn't the other people that he victimized be speaking up with me? In the days leading up to the meeting I became aware from Regina that Lyle had sexually assaulted at least three other women in the family including her. There was only one thing that needed to be done and that was to call the police but instead, I made my way to the living room, my legs shaking as I walked.

I enter the room to see my father leaning on the armrest of the L-shaped couch. He is sitting with his body slightly forward with his arms crossed, staring at Lyle. To my right and in the corner of the couch is Lyle looking at his hands. I look at them too, feeling them on my body as though he's touching me right then and there. My cousin Regina is behind me sitting against the other armrest of the couch. I look down at the floor. The wood shutters are drawn but there are random slivers of sunlight on the carpet and walls. The room is dimly lit by a few table lamps and the television is off. I stand there staring at the contrast of my bare feet against the cream-coloured carpet still not having the faintest idea of what I was going to say. My toes are freezing courtesy of the AC and I want to scream as I am angry at myself for feeling small and weak. I do not feel in a position of power and am exasperated and embarrassed with the efforts of my family. I'm sure Lyle knew he was getting away with it but there was nothing I could do except feel the blood thumping in my ears as I stood there trying to formulate a sentence in my mind to utter in front of my father. I wanted someone to call the police. I never wanted to see Lyle again. I wanted to protect my family from this monster, but I could not accomplish any of that. Why didn't anyone care? He sexually assaulted me and instead of calling the police, we were simply going to talk and then what...? Suddenly I hear my dad's voice "Okay, say what you want to say."

I look up and the room is quiet and waiting for me to say something. I spit out "I don't want you to touch me ever again." Lyle looks up at me and then back down to his hands. "I'm sorry I made you feel that way," he responds.

I want to rip his tongue out of his mouth. How dare he apologize in such a dismissive manner as though I had misunderstood what he was trying to do over and over and over again for four years. "You know exactly what you did," I say, trying to control my rage and beginning to shake. "Don't touch me ever again. Do you understand?" I say.

"Yes of course," Lyle responds, "I understand." Again, there is silence and I feel my body shaking. I wished him dead with all of my being and pictured him on the ground while I kicked his face into the back of his skull. I hated him, hated what he did to me and hated my family for putting me into the situation I was in.

"Do you want to say anything else?" asked my dad. "No," I reply. I turn away quickly and leave the room without uttering another word.

"What did you say to him?" my mother asks pulling me aside. "I told him never to touch me again," I respond angrily. She looks at me surprised. *Did she expect me to come sailing out of that room without a care in the world? Where is my mother? Where is the woman that is supposed to protect me?* I look into her eyes pleading for a sign that she sees me, but she stares right back clearly confused with my hostility. I don't know who she is anymore, and I feel as though my heart is physically breaking. It is hard to breathe as I look into her face wondering who this person is in place of my mother. Where is my mother? I feel as though I have lost my mother while I stare at the doppelganger in front of me.

I spend the rest of the time in Florida reading books and watching TV without engaging in too much conversation. I can't wait to leave so that I can be back in my room, back with my friends and far away from the senseless environment I was in.

I did not see Lyle again on that trip and my parents and I left for Canada a few days later.

THREE

HIT & RUN

"I really don't want to go," I told my parents. "Do I have to go?"

"Yes, you have to go," my mother answered looking at me confused. "You can't stay home alone. We are all going. It's a family event." My dad looked up at me and I turned towards my brothers, but they were busy eating dinner. *Why didn't anyone get it?* I thought. *Why is everyone acting like nothing happened? Why on earth is my dad not reacting? Why doesn't anyone understand that what he did was a big deal? Is there something wrong with me? Is that why I was the only one that spoke up? What did I do wrong?* "Don't worry," my dad says. "You will be safe. He won't come near you." I feel myself starting to tremble and look down at my plate, stabbing pieces of salad with my fork in an attempt to steady my hands. Hearing the word *safe* instantly nauseated me. I certainly did not feel safe and did not trust everyone else's definition of safe as it made no sense to me. I continued eating so that I could move on with the clean-up and be alone in my room. I was raging inside.

I could not believe the audacity of my father telling me

I'll be safe. What was done the last time I needed help? Absolutely nothing. My father wasn't going to keep me safe, and neither was my mother or the rest of the family. What did they expect me to do? Say hello to him as though nothing was wrong? How could I pretend that he didn't have his hands all over me? How can I even look at him without remembering the absolute terror of waking up in the middle of the night with him in my room? How can I act normally when all I see when I look at him, are snapshots of what he did to me playing on a loop. He assaulted me. He violated me. He abused me. Sure, my mother didn't know every gory little detail. *But she knew enough,* I thought.

I didn't want to see him and that was the agreement established and the promise that was made to me when I went to Florida for the mock trial. I was promised I would never have to see him again and less than six months later my family decides to break their promise to me and show me that it is more important to celebrate an event and to pretend we are a family, than to ensure the safety of my mental and physical health. I could not stand the hypocrisy that oozed from everyone around me. My family was not a family. I had no real family. It made me physically ill each day. I loathed everyone around me and felt repulsion towards my parents. It was as though everyone took a vow of silence regarding the abuse and whatever happened magically vanished. The only boundary that was created between my family and my Aunt Bianca's family was that I was never to discuss the abuse with my cousin Tamara and that I was to be kept away from Lyle.

It was obvious what I felt and what happened to me was irrelevant and unimportant to everyone and life was going to continue the way it always did, with a few annual visits a year to the US and Italy and no regard to how I felt about seeing my perpetrator. My family had zero understanding that they had set me up to be traumatized again and again, directly and indirectly by Lyle and everyone else that was too afraid to face the reality of the situation. This was the prison that I got locked into, without committing a crime and without any sign of a release date. The food I was fed were morsels of love and what I was given to drink flooded my body with shame. The new reality scared me, and I was scared to go to Florida again. The only reason he did not rape me was because I got away from him. He had been grooming me for four years and the last few times that he had sexually assaulted me, his attempts at raping me would have succeeded had I not gotten away from him. I had to find a way to protect myself since it was clear no one was going to help me, but I had no idea how to do that.

The color of the water seems to be a bluish green. I am standing by the edge of my Aunt Bianca's pool looking at the décor floating gently in the water. There are other guests outside, but I am standing alone. It is a nice night, and some people begin to go home. There are a few rooms in the house that are now empty, and my perpetrator is still there, somewhere close by. Safety in numbers, I think, he can't do anything to me in front of other people. I am scared and have been all night knowing how close he is in vicinity to me. I am baffled and angry that my parents and family have abandoned me, placing me right back into a situation where Lyle has full access to me. My body is tense, and I am scared.

Outside near the pool with others I feel safe so that is where I decide to stand as the celebration thins out and people head home. My family and I are returning to Canada in a few days and this event would be the only time Lyle and

I would be in the same location. The entire night I did everything I could to stay away from him and succeeded in doing so. I felt like I was on the home stretch and in just a few days I'd be far away and safe from him.

Suddenly, out of the corner of my eye I see him walking towards me. My throat closes and I stand motionless on high alert. As he walks by me, I hear him hiss in my direction, "You didn't tell them you liked it you slut. Why didn't you tell them that part?" My eyes well up with tears as soon as I hear his voice. My body freezes and I start to tremble. What on earth was he talking about? Enjoyed it? What the hell what he thinking? He was the most disgusting, vile creature I had ever encountered. He was a monster. Before I have a chance to recover from the first atrocity out of his mouth, he walks by again, leans in my direction and adds, "You know you liked it. Just admit it you whore." I stand there in disbelief and quickly look around to see if anyone heard him. As usual, no one is nearby. I hang my head and turn away from him. He has gone again into the house and now I can't go to the bathroom and collect myself in case I run into him. I have nowhere to go and nowhere to hide. I am trapped. Again. A minute later I see him across the patio laughing and smiling with other family members. People that are aware or heard whispers of his behavior towards me. He catches my gaze and smiles at me wickedly. I feel like I'm in a nightmare, but I can't wake up. My legs start to shake as I walk past him into the house and lock myself in the bathroom. The rest of the evening I try my best to hide from him, but he finds me and continues his verbal psychological assault on me. I never thought I'd feel him hunt for me again. I try to hide but everywhere I turn there he is either smiling and laughing with family members and guests or discretely launching another verbal assault on me.

Finally, the party ends and all the guests including Lyle, leave to go home. I cry myself to sleep that night knowing full well that despite what he did before, and despite what he continues to do, I have no one to help me and I am alone.

I came home from the trip enraged and in complete shock. I could not for the life of me understand why my parents would put me into a situation like that. Deeper and deeper my wound grew with each unseized opportunity my family had to help me. I had gone to them for help, and they had shown me their ridiculous solutions. Day by day I sank deeper into self-loathing and shame, and I could feel myself unraveling.

The issues I had as a child with anxiety were now much bigger problems as they had now developed into panic disorder, and I was having panic attacks a few times a week. Each attack left me exhausted, shaky and feeling very fragile and at times the attack would be so intense that they would leave me on the floor writhing in pain with each movement of my body feeling like torture. Each breath I would take felt like someone was squeezing my throat. These were the panic attacks that I would scream for my mother, and she would come running to where I was. If I didn't have the energy to call for her, I would crawl on my hands and knees to wherever she was. I would tell her that I wanted to die, that this pain was going to kill me, and she would wrap her arms around me to help me feel better. Sometimes she'd cry too while I would rock back and forth and moan in agony. I hated that I needed my mother during those intense episodes. On the one hand I wanted my mother to help me and comfort me, but deep down I hated her for not helping me with the abuse. At night I would be plagued by disturbing dreams, nightmares or sleep paralysis. In my dreams I'd be running from someone or something but could never get away. I had regular, recurring nightmares of being raped. I had panic attacks in my sleep and sometimes would wake up to myself biting my wrists or hands. I became afraid of everything inside of me but appeared fearless and confident on the outside. No one knew any of this was happening.

To deal with my internal struggles I began to engage in violent and impulsive behavior as well as self-harm. I was cutting myself on different parts of my body as the pain would enable me to focus on something else besides my internal struggle. Somehow, cutting helped me deal with the internal chaos and the physical manifestations of stress I was experiencing. I could not explain what was going on inside me to cause such intense episodes of panic and pain, but I could certainly look at a cut, point at where the pain was and feel like I understood where it was coming from.

My outlet and the person I spoke about the situation the most to was my high school boyfriend. I had met Joel at an amusement park when I was fourteen and became inseparable quickly thereafter. He was kind, gentle, incredibly smart, and hilariously funny. He had a passion for the arts and lived with his mother in an old warehouse building in downtown Toronto. His world was so different from mine. He was free to do as he pleased and in his free time created all kinds of things. He made sculptures, practiced music, wrote poetry or stories, and read books. I had never met anyone like him. My world was so structured and felt so heavy. His life, or rather the way I experienced life with him, made me feel less heavy and not ashamed of myself. He reminded me of all the things I liked, but had managed to forget while trying to survive my life and family. The first time I walked into the warehouse, I stared in awe at my surroundings. Everything around me looked fascinating. His mother's various art pieces and supplies would be strewn about depending on what medium she was working on, and there always were so many books everywhere. The warehouse was warm and inviting despite the 20-foot ceilings and huge windows. There were no walls inside the space whatsoever and the rooms would be separated by furniture placement or décor. The door to his room was a set of long heavy curtains and his wardrobe was an old soda pop vending machine that had been hollowed out and set up on the interior like a closet. It was all so refreshing from the life I was living at home. I shared everything with him about me and my life including the abuse and how my family was dealing with it.

When I returned from Florida and let him know what had happened, he insisted I tell my family what Lyle had done this time but I didn't care to.

"What are you talking about? How is what he said to you not important?" Joel asked. "Of course your parents will care about what he said."

"Why would they?" I replied. "Nothing was done after he put his hands on me so why would they do anything now?" Joel was quiet and then said firmly, "It doesn't matter. You should tell them anyway." I didn't care what he thought. I had no intention of telling anyone. I did not trust my family as I was certain they'd put me into a situation I didn't want to be in ever again.

I felt defeated and exhausted and to ignore the issue, I self-harmed more frequently by closing my eyes while driving or getting in the way of cars too. The cutting made me feel physically more in control of my life since I was the one creating my own pain. I would almost go into a daze while cutting and feel a rush of happiness when I saw blood. The habit was becoming hard to hide and I would lie to whomever asked about my injuries. As far as everyone else knew I was clumsy and injured myself quite frequently. I was skipping classes on a regular basis and frequently smoking marijuana. The weed would calm my nerves and help me feel relaxed. It would make me laugh and feel like the world wasn't so scary. It gave me a method to find sleep and tranquility in a body full of chaos and I was able to focus more effectively on reading and writing. I wrote a lot and carried notebooks with me wherever I went. It was my only method to extract the poison from my wounds. The weed helped me relax, but it did not stop me from cutting and did not stop the psycho-emotional rollercoaster I was on.

"I don't understand what's wrong. Why can't you just tell me what's wrong so that I can help you?" Rob looked at me his eyes pleading for me to open up. I look at him and shake my head. I am standing in front of my friend Rob with my back against the brick wall of the park office. We were having a perfectly good day skipping school until Rob started pressing me about why I've been so quiet lately and why I'm sad all the time.

I met Rob in the first few months of high school in French class. He sat near me and we fell into the same group of friends that I had befriended as well. Rob was also of Italian background and was familiar with the dynamics of my home. We found common ground as he had his own set of issues at home, but while I confided in him about my home life and family, I never told him about the abuse.

"There is nothing wrong that can't be fixed. I'm having issues with my mother, and they'll go away soon enough," I answer.

"What does that mean? What's wrong? What is happening? What issues are you talking about?"

"You know what? Leave me alone. How about that? How about you do what I ask? I don't need your help. I'm fine. Everything is fine. I'm done with this conversation," I say as I step away from him. He blocks my path and I lean back against the wall. I begin to laugh nervously. "Okay, brave star," I say, "let me through."

"Not until you tell me what's wrong," Rob says firmly.

"Fuck you," I respond looking directly into his eyes.

"Fuck you," he replies in the same manner.

I drop my gaze and shake my head while taking a deep breath. "Please get out of my way," I say to Rob's shoes. I raise my head and look at Rob again. He does not move. I raise my arms to push him out of my way and Rob grabs my forearms to stop me. I yelp in pain as his grip opens up every cut on both my arms, all at once. I whimper as he loosens his grip and can't see through my tears as he lifts one of my sleeves up to look at my arm. He looks at me in disbelief, "What are you doing, honey?" he asked. "What did you do?" I begin to cry as he pulls me closer to give me a hug and I cry in his arms like an infant. He lets me cry and hugs me until I pull away from him. He did not ask me again what was wrong, but he did remain close to me for the rest of the scholastic year letting me know there was a first aid kit in his locker if I needed it. I would use the kit and notice that each time I used something it would quickly be replaced.

I wanted to die, but I was too scared to carry out a suicide. Everyday living took every ounce of energy I had. I felt exhausted and hopeless and did not see any type of future that I wanted to be a part of. If this was going to be my life, I didn't want it.

Eventually I decided I was leaving home. I could not bear to live a lifetime within a family unit that did not protect me or that thought in some universe, the abuse could be ignored. I was embarrassed I came from a family that condoned Lyle's behaviour and I could not help but wonder what life was going to look like down the road. *What's it going to be like thirty years from now? Will the lie still be intact?* I pictured our entire family at a dinner table clinking glasses and enjoying a special meal together and my stomach would turn. It wasn't hard to do so since I had already seen him carrying on with my own eyes as if he had done nothing to me. He had children with my cousin and the thought of him doing something to his own children haunted me. I could not imagine having to witness and play the part in a lifetime of lies to protect someone like him. I could not wrap my head around why no one was taking the situation seriously. *He would have raped me then and there in the kitchen if I hadn't gotten away.* I was so let down and hurt, wondering why everyone turned their back on me.

The only thing that made sense to me was leaving home yet Joel would not entertain any discussion involving me running away and living on the streets. "Where are you going to go?" he asked on the phone one night. "I don't know," I responded, "I am done here. No one gives a shit about what he did, and I won't ignore it."

"Okay, but I'm sure if you told your parents what he did on this trip something would change," Joel said.

"Stop saying that. You don't get it. They don't care and I'm tired of you not listening to me. You don't live here. You don't know what it's like."

Joel relented and a few days later asked me to come by his place. His mother sat me down and explained that I needn't run away and that I could live there if I wanted to. I did not want to live with my boyfriend and his mother, but understood it was safer than being homeless. Nina gave me a hug, made some tea, and we talked about what it would be like for me to live there. She made it clear that she was taking me in whether I remained her son's significant other or not. "If you break up," she said, "You will still have a home and I will always care for you." When the subject of schooling was discussed I let her know that I wasn't doing badly in school but did not have the median average to enter university anymore. "You'll need to get your grades back up. Lucky for you I can help with that," she said with a smile. "As for the costs, we will cross that bridge when we come to it." Nina wanted me to understand I was safe and secure, and understand that I would not lose the opportunity for a higher education if I left home. I cried in her arms feeling relief and a tinge of hopefulness to think that soon I would be stepping into a new life. I felt safer already.

Since I was not yet eighteen, she asked that upon arrival, I quickly visit the local police station to inform them that I was not missing and that I was safe. I agreed and thought about our discussion on the way home.

I felt that the living arrangement would work and was excited about the fact that schooling wasn't out of the question if I left home. In what felt like another life, I had wanted to become a writer, but I saw the dream moving further and further away from me. My mind was lost in the labyrinth of manipulation, lies and gaslighting from my family and all I wanted to do was untangle myself from the toxic web in which I was ensnared. I needed to be around people that I felt safe with and did not want to be part of a family in which abuse seemed rampant, and accepted. My body was already feeling better knowing the end was near. I knew I'd see my family again eventually, but at least I didn't have to see him and endure his torture. He would never have access to me again and knowing that in my bones felt glorious.

A few days later, I left my house in the middle of the night running barefoot to Joel's car. The plan was for me to pack my clothes into bed sheets and to leave them at the side of the house, but I only made a few trips up and down the stairs before I decided to get out fast.

"What are you doing?" Joel whispers urgently to me as he sees me standing at the side of my house. "Go get the rest of your stuff!"

"No, I'm good," I respond. "I'm ready to go."

"Please just go in one more time to grab a few more things," he says. I run inside the house and quietly make my way back up the stairs avoiding the creaky top step. I walk into my room and look around. It is a complete disaster and quite obvious that I was not going to make any sense of what to take. I speed quickly back down the stairs and run to Joel's car jumping into his passenger seat. "You didn't take anything else?" he says while looking at me. "No. Let's just GO," I say. Joel looks into the backseat to his friend that tagged along to help us and shrugged his shoulders. Adam shrugged back and Joel started the car.

I had to leave the house. I knew I didn't bring a lot with me, but I didn't care. I was terrified someone would wake up and cause a terrible scene or worse, call the police. The anxiety in my stomach felt as though I had an imaginary switchblade sticking out of it and someone kept moving the blade clockwise, and then counterclockwise. Once we arrived at Joel's, we dropped my belongings off and got back into the car. We drove to the police station, and I personally informed them I was not a missing person and handed them my photo. The police took my name and information and let me know that they had already been notified that I had been reported missing. I sighed and shook my head. "No, I'm not missing. I ran away from home, and I have a safe place to stay." I signed a document and left the police station. I could not wait to get back to the house. I was exhausted and needed sleep so badly I felt nauseous. Unfortunately, my anxiety got the better of me and after lying down for maybe forty-five seconds my insides turned inside out, and I ran into the bathroom vomiting a few times into the toilet before lying down on the cold floor trying to bring the temperature of my body down. I stared at the ceiling, tears streaming down my face. I felt completely broken, worthless and ashamed. After a few minutes I sit up cross-legged, leaning against the tub. I look around the bathroom and see a razor in the shower. *No. Not now. It is not the time. You are safe now,* I think to myself.

When I open the door I see Joel sitting in a chair waiting for me. Mortified and ashamed that he had somewhat witnessed my episode I did not meet his eyes and slowly walked back to my new room. I felt small and powerless over my disorder, exactly like everything else in my life at that point. I had no idea how to stop the attacks or lessen them or do anything at all to control them and they just kept getting more and more intense. I lay down in bed and closed my eyes trying to sink into the mattress beneath me.

I woke up to the sound of the phone ringing. I open my eyes and for a second forget where I am. Nina had kept the phone off the hook when we arrived home from the police station so that I could try to settle down and sleep. My parents figured out where I was and reached out to some of my friends to pass along messages for me to come home, but I let them know it wasn't happening. As the day wore on my parents, more specifically my mother, became more frantic. According to her, if I stayed there for the night it would insinuate that I had engaged in sex with Joel. Why this was of such importance I could not comprehend. My mother's preoccupation with any consensual sexual behavior I engaged in, should be the least of her concerns. What she should be worried about was that there was a sexual predator in the family.

News of my midnight run reached my dad's brothers and sisters living nearby. Where had I gone? Why had I done this? My parents informed whoever asked, that Joel and his mother brainwashed me into running away since my parents did not want us to date. There was never any mention of the abuse I endured or the tragedy of their inaction. How could they be so blind to not see how I was being impacted? A week before my mother and I had to be pulled apart during an argument. How could they just turn away from it all? My departure also gave ammunition to anyone that did not want to face the truth regarding the abuse. It was as though there was a smear campaign created against me in which my family all agreed I was mentally ill, promiscuous, and my words could not be trusted. They painted it as though Joel and his mother wanted me as their own and that I was not mentally stable enough to make correct decisions for myself. I guess the latter was accurate, but it wasn't because of Joel or his mother.

As day turned into evening, my parents passed the message along to me through a friend that a hotel room was booked nearby and if I could please sleep there to calm my mother's nerves. I felt the request was ridiculous but in the end, I accepted thinking it was the first step to working together towards the resolution of many issues. My friend Grace was at the hotel, and we talked about my recent departure and the current climate between me and my family.

"Your parents are convinced that Joel's mother tricked you or something happened where you could not make proper decisions," Grace told me. I shake my head at her and smile.

"They know why I left even if they pretend they don't," I reply. "And yes, I am not permitted to see Joel but that is only a minor reason as to why I left." We are on the hotel balcony while I smoke a cigarette. I feel more and more defeated with each nugget of information Grace tells me regarding her conversations with my parents. It makes me sick to know they are pretending not to understand what caused my exit. *How long is this going to be hidden?* I think. *How long is this charade going to go on for?* A few days after the hotel and staying overnight at Grace's house. I went back home in hopes that my parents and I would talk and iron out all of the misunderstandings.

When I walked through the door my mother thanked me for coming back. I look at her with no expression and made my way up the stairs to my room, opening the door to see several of my things scattered about. I knew I had left a mess but could tell someone else had been rifling through my room and through my things. I feel violated, powerless and fall asleep hoping that one day soon I would not wake up.

It took less than twenty-four hours before I understood that my homecoming meant something completely different to my parents than it did for me. I wanted to have honest discussions about issues and come to resolutions with them, but they were not interested. We discussed my running away and I realized that my parents wanted me to avoid my 'toxic' boyfriend and his mother. They weren't interested in two-way communication and weren't interested in what I had to say. I was back and that was it. That was all they cared about. As they spoke and reprimanded me for leaving, my mind wandered off and I made the decision to leave once I turned eighteen in less than a year. Immediately once the thought entered my mind I felt a spark of light in my heart. *Maybe I'll survive all of this,* I think. *Maybe if I use the time between now and my 18th birthday I'll be ready. I am not going to fall asleep and never wake up. I'm going to plan my exit.* I gave myself comfort by thinking of the different things I would have to do to prepare, like saving money and figuring out which neighborhood I wanted to live in. I knew I needed to be away from them and in control of my life and safety if I was to feel better and move on.

I mostly hid in my room reading and writing to pass time. My mother was travelling to the beach house that summer and I did not want to go but Joel and I had been arguing since he had dropped me off at the hotel a few days earlier and our relationship was essentially broken. Both our lives had been turned upside down by the recent events and it seemed to him like I had chosen the other side. He was disappointed and angry with me, and I felt guilty for pulling him and his mother into the situation. I was so ashamed that I had gone back to something I had so desperately ran away from. I didn't choose the other side I chose the easy way out as I was exhausted from all the fighting coming at me from every angle. I became caught in a cycle of hating my parents and family for not protecting me, and doing things the way they wanted in hopes of gaining acceptance, love and trust. I saw Joel before I left for Italy, but nothing was resolved and we were neither together, nor broken up. We said good bye and we felt it.

Because I travelled to Italy so often, I had a group of friends as well as cousins that I would spend time with when visiting. The first few weeks I slept a lot and didn't interact much with anyone. I felt as though I was a visitor in my own body. I would sit and stare into space, count the tiles on the terrace or stare up at the sky watching the clouds roll by. I was completely drained, felt dead inside and nothing seemed real. When I started feeling a bit more alive, I began going out with my cousins or friends. I had occasionally exchanged letters with a boy named Luca, whom I met a few summers before, and over time began confiding in him when we would all go out.

Luca was disgusted with Lyle and couldn't understand how my family could turn their backs on me and protect him. There was nothing he could do, and he knew that, so he helped by being there any time to talk. My cousin Anna had come home to the beach house from university in Florence for the summer. We had a three-year age gap between us which made her the female cousin closest to me in age. I opened up to her and explained everything that happened from the time the abuse started to the current events that led me to the conversation I was having with her in that moment. My cousin was in complete shock. She too had heard the story that I was somehow brainwashed or had become mentally ill while dating my boyfriend. She had no idea of the abuse but understood completely why I had left home. She validated my feelings and was angry that everything had gotten so incredibly twisted trying to protect the family portrait. It was such a relief to feel support from her.

"Does Tamara know?" she asked me.

"I have no idea what she knows but she does know he

touched me in a manner he shouldn't have. She never asked me and I'm not sure what my mother or Aunt Bianca told her," I responded. "I'm not permitted to speak with her about the subject and nor do I have a desire to at this point. If she asks I'll tell her but I'm tired of fighting."

Anna looks at me and nods. "Yes. That makes sense," she said.

———

"What are you reading?" my mother asked. I look up to see her leaning on the terrace railing. It is a hot afternoon, and I am instantly perturbed by her interruption. "A book," I respond. She takes a seat near me and begins to talk about going home in the next two weeks. I am not overly engaged in the conversation and mutter that the last place I want to be is back at home with them. She looks at me with the usual *you are being difficult* face and moves on. I roll my eyes and take a deep breath to settle myself. My mother's presence angered me.

"What about here?" she asks. "Do you like it here?"

"What do you mean *what about here*? I'm not staying here for the winter if that is what you mean." I look at her confused. *The town has one stoplight and there isn't even a high school in the town.*

"I mean why not stay in Italy and go to school here?" she said. I look at her blankly.

"You can go to Florence with your cousin and complete your last year of high school there."

"Ya, I'm sure you'll leave me alone here." I roll my eyes and return to my book.

"Yes. You can live with your cousin and her roommates. While they attend university, you'll attend your last year of high school. If you like it, you can stay for university as well."

"Did you tell Dad about this?" I ask looking up at her.

"Don't worry about your dad. He won't be an issue if you want to stay."

I look past her towards the ocean. I can feel myself wanting to cry but hold back tears. *Why don't they want me around anymore? Am I that problematic and unlovable? Why don't they want me back at home? Sure, I ran away but they were permitting the abuse to continue. Why? Why is what he did okay?* I feel utterly defeated. I don't want to stay but I don't want to go home either. I feel numb.

I think to myself that there may have been conversations recently to discuss my next steps without my input. My family would not have come up with this idea without discussing it first. I wished those discussions would have resulted in helping me and not sending me away. Never did I anticipate this turn of events. I take a breath and close my eyes. I see an image of walking back into my house an ocean away and feel my stomach twist. A moment later the words fall out of my mouth. "Sure," I respond colorlessly. "I'll stay."

FOUR
FIRENZE

A sliver of orange sun was on the horizon of a giant sunflower field. As dawn broke, I watched mesmerized at the landscape whipping by. I was lying stomach down on a sleeper in an overnight train my parents and I had taken from Calabria to Florence. I had my headphones on the entire night listening to the Cranberries, *No Need to Argue* album on repeat. The train trip from Calabria to Florence was long, and instead of taking a train during the day, we took a night train scheduled to arrive to Florence by morning. I didn't sleep much and for some reason did not believe they were going to leave me in Florence and travel back to Canada. I had never seen the city before and the school system was pretty different than the Canadian one I was used to. Everything was all very sudden and felt surreal.

My cousin Anna had left a few weeks before my parents and I, so she would be waiting at the apartment when we arrived. I would be sharing a room with her, and living in the apartment with three other roommates. I was nervous and happy to be living away from my parents but the sadness, worthlessness, shame and anger I continued to feel inside weighed me down. The cutting had become less frequent in the summer as I was unable to hide it, but I found that as long as I stayed away from most of my family members, I physically and mentally felt better. After I told Luca I was staying we thought that maybe what we were feeling for each other could be explored. In my heart I missed Joel, but I knew it was over and I felt a new life was beginning. Luca and I got along, and he understood me. He was warm, caring and we took care of each other. He and other friends were also attending universities nearby so I had a small group I could connect with.

As the scenery sped by, the rising light gave way to more landscape. I saw farmhouses nestled within rolling velvety hills and tall cedars lining the long winding driveways to the farmhouses. As the train continued to charge forward, the landscape changed again. Low level apartments alongside small villas started to appear and become closer together. All the homes had terracotta roofs and were coloured a beautiful fiery orange tile that seemed to compliment the rising sun. I was in awe with how picturesque everything looked. The rising of the sun reminded me of a story I once read where a music conductor would conduct the orchestra that colored each day. The scenery looked like a painting and as we arrived closer to our stop I started to feel better and also excited that I'd be living in such a pretty place. *And if it was horrible I could always disappear into the fold*, I thought. *Or take a trip back to Canada never to be seen again*. I close my eyes for a moment and take a deep breath exhaling silently and slowly. I was trying hard to stay positive, yet the intrusive thoughts were still there at all times just bouncing around in my head. I could never live in the moment. It was next to impossible to just be. I open my eyes again to the scenery out of the window. Maybe this was the place that I needed to be at that moment in my life. I had no doubt of this as I watched the sun climb into the sky to light up the world I would soon be living in.

"Firenze Campo Di Marte, prossima fermata, Campo di Marte," said a pleasant feminine voice on the loudspeaker. My parents and I were standing near the exit door and ready to leave the train at our scheduled stop. As we pulled into the station, I looked for my cousin Anna and saw her on the platform waiting with a smile. We headed over to the apartment and spent the next two weeks preparing for my scholastic year. I enrolled into high school, bought some supplies and books needed for my courses, and familiarized myself with the city and transit system with my cousin and parents and sometimes Luca when he'd visit on the weekends. My school was in the historical center of Florence which was also close to the University if I wanted to meet up with my cousin to grab a bite to eat or take the bus home together. I was feeling increasingly comfortable and more myself. My anger towards my parents was subsiding to tolerance and I looked forward to their departure.

Living in Florence was like a beautiful dream. I had only been to one Italian city to date and that was Rome so there was an expectation in my mind that Rome and Florence would be similar. After my train ride into the city though, I realized that my assumption was deeply inaccurate. Rome was a beautiful place, but Florence in my eyes was breathtaking. Everywhere I turned looked like a portrait of something or other. In late fall when the weather changed, I loved being in the city after the rain. The streets would be barren of people and the dark cobblestones would be shiny and wet as if they had just been polished. The first time I walked into Piazza della Signoria from Via delle Calzaiuoli I stood there speechless, staring at the enormous piazza, centuries-old stone buildings, and the outdoor museum. I could not believe I was living in a city that was so beautiful. At night churches and cathedrals would be lit up against the darkness and they were as striking to see at night, as they were during the day. I loved everything about Florence and felt confident that this was the city I was meant to live in. It was a very odd feeling for me, but it was there, nonetheless. Florence felt like home almost immediately, as though I had returned from a long trip despite never being there before then.

School was much different just as I had thought. Some of the courses I was taking included Art History and Italian Literature which were subjects I had never taken before. I studied Machiavelli, the Medici's, the history of Italian language, Dante Alighieri, and the socio-political environment of 15th century renaissance Florence. I liked what they taught in school. It was interesting and so refreshing to learn things that were entirely new. I would learn about Michelangelo's David and then walk across the street to see the actual sculpture as well as his entire opera of art that included The David. If I wasn't in museums or churches, I would wander the streets for hours listening to music and pretending I was a tourist. I was homesick sometimes, especially in the beginning as I felt completely thrown away by my family, but I made the best of the opportunity I had, and it was there I understood the importance of how a beautiful environment can help your mindset when you are trying to heal. I made friends at school and would sometimes walk through the city streets with them. After school we would occasionally head to Fortezza Da Basso and hang out in the sun until we felt like heading home. I had also met a girl in class that lived close to my apartment, and she introduced me to some of her neighborhood friends as well. Some evenings, I would hang out with them in a 13th century church courtyard down the street from my house. The people I met helped me learn Italian and would tease me when I made mistakes. I didn't care, it was all good fun and it helped me learn the language more quickly. I did not make any English-speaking friends so by the time the Christmas holidays came along a few months later, my Italian had improved significantly and felt more comfortable conversing with people in Italian. Luca's father noticed it when we arrived home for the holidays, and I was pretty proud of myself. My brain was working with what seemed like less fog inside of it, so it was easier to absorb things.

With all the wonder and magic around me, with my new mask on, I did my best to immerse myself in the present but found it to be more and more challenging as time went on. Although I loved where I lived, was having fewer panic attacks and nightmares, deep down I felt incredibly sad to be 7,000 km away from everyone I knew. I loved Florence and the freedom of doing what I pleased. It came at a high price though and I still felt abandoned by my family wondering why they chose to protect a sexual deviant and not me. I cried most days and nights when I was alone. I missed everything. I missed my friends, I missed Grace, I missed my room, I missed television shows in English, and missed so many odd things that didn't make sense. I missed light switches, water taps and stores that were not designated for one specific thing. I missed Canadian coffee and candies that weren't available in Italy like jawbreakers. I missed the regularity of seeing pancake mix, maple syrup and peanut butter in the supermarket. I missed turkey and Thanksgiving and missed the Canadian fall season. I missed the sound of the dial tone when you would pick up the phone to call out, I missed hearing English being spoken and whenever I would hear it in the streets, I would perk up, but then instantly feel my heart break too. The ache of solitude would not change too much throughout my days and nights.

Another way to cope was helping English speaking tourists find their way around the city or give them advice on things to see. I pretended I was happy when I was talking to strangers and would give people the impression that I came from a well-to-do family that sent me to boarding school. Everyone believed the lies, including me. One afternoon while wandering about I saw someone I knew from my high school in Canada. She was older than me, but we had hung out several times in the same circle of friends.

"Alina! What are you doing here?" I exclaimed.

"Rosemary! How are you? What are YOU doing here?" Alina laughed. We gave each other a hug and I heard her map crumple between us. "Oh shoot!" Alina says.

"It's okay. It didn't rip," I say looking down at the city map she had of Florence. "How are you? What are you doing here? Are you alone?" I ask.

"I'm good! I'm on vacation and yes I'm alone. Are you on vacation too?" Alina asked excitedly.

"No actually. I live here now," I say.

"In Florence?"

"'Yes. It's maybe a ten-minute bus ride from downtown. I moved here to finish school."

"Wow," Alina says. "That's incredible. Are you in school now? Is it a Canadian school?"

"No. I'm in an Italian school too!" I reply with a smile.

"My Italian has definitely improved!" I add. "So, what about you?" I ask.

"Oh, I was here for a few days, but leaving tomorrow to visit Rome before heading to Toronto, but I can't find the currency office noted on this map to get some cash."

I helped her find a currency exchange office and she told me how jealous she was that I was living in such a beautiful place. I smiled and completely agreed with her that Florence was enchanting and let her believe that I was happy in my heart. We hugged each other good bye and I wished her a safe trip back home. The encounter made me incredibly melancholy and homesick, however, I was proud of myself that I didn't show her, and she didn't see how emotionally devastated I was. As I travelled home that day the beat of *Blood Makes Noise* by Suzanne Vega danced in my headphones.

On the surface I embodied my new life but inside I had given up. I didn't speak of the abuse, how it made me feel and how the nightmares continued or how much I fought the urge to disappear. I fantasized constantly about taking off and starting a new life alone, indulging in some of my intrusive thoughts with a cut or two, but I did not have the courage or strength to go through with a plan. I was tired of fighting, and I was lost. I felt detached and disassociated from myself. Since Luca was so far away my marijuana habit was easy to maintain. I knew he looked down at people that smoked it so I never told him I did. I smoked during the week with my friends at school and drank heavily on the weekends. My body felt like I had a tornado stuck inside of it and was trying to get out. The anger I felt towards my parents made me sick. I felt ashamed and embarrassed that others might see how completely worthless I was if my own parents didn't want me around.

In the meantime, to make matters more complicated, when I began dating Luca, people he knew were approaching him and telling him I was trouble. I'm sure they heard I had run away, and I really didn't expect much from a small Calabrian town, but it angered me that Luca had to deal with it. He came from a wealthy family, and I was seen as the trash trying to remove him or dislodge him somehow from his privileged life. I was embarrassed to know that he was being questioned and could not even imagine what people were saying about me behind closed doors. I knew that small town talk was just that, yet it pulled my self-esteem down even further. One day I was sure I wasn't going to be good enough for Luca either, just like I wasn't good enough for my parents.

And then came the dissection. "Ti dobbiamo operare," the doctor said. "What?" I responded in Italian.

"We need to operate on you," he repeated in Italian more slowly. I felt like someone hit me in the face with a steel bat. *Operare?* I thought. *That meant surgery.* "When?" I asked the doctor. He looked at me and said, "Now, soon, once we are organized, we need to operate. Probably in the next hour or so. The nurse will be in to help you prepare for surgery," he quickly said after realizing I spoke Italian. With that said, he met my eyes and gave me a quick nod. I stared back with nothing to say. He waited a moment and disappeared behind a door. I sat in the room alone waiting for a stranger to prepare me for surgery. I was terrified. A few minutes later an older nurse comes into the room and orders me to undress without taking her eyes off the cabinet as she enters the room. She faces the cabinet and begins removing bottles from the shelves and placing them on the countertop below. I stand up to do so and I'm shaking. The nurse puts her hand on my shoulder, but I don't see it coming and jump out of my skin. "It's okay," she says with her hand still on my shoulder, "You are going to be okay." I smile at her and begin to tear up. I need her hand off my shoulder immediately or I feel I will go crazy. The memory of Lyle's hands make me feel repulsion towards human touch yet in that moment, I needed comfort so much it hurt. Silent tears fall from my face as the nurse helps me prepare for the surgery. I was very quiet and only spoke a few words when asked. I was doing everything they were asking, and the hospital staff was kind, but I was so afraid, and the tears did not stop falling until I was given something to help me settle down.

My stomach had been aching for days, but I thought that it was something I ate or my nerves acting up again, so I didn't tell anyone I wasn't feeling well. Unfortunately, after a few days of pain that was not going away, my cousin called a doctor that made house calls to examine my stomach. I was in bed when he arrived to the apartment, and he was led into my room by my cousin. He asked if he could examine my belly and pressed down gently in different places to determine any issues. As soon as he pressed down on my lower right side I yelped in pain, almost losing consciousness. The doctor looked at my cousin and told her to take me to the hospital immediately as it seemed as though I had acute appendicitis. He couldn't understand how I had I was still attending school and going about my days with the pain he figured I was experiencing. He looked at me and I shrugged my shoulders. "I don't know," I said in Italian while he stared at me puzzled. One of my roommates appeared a second later at my door and in less than five minutes I was on my way to the hospital in the front seat of my roommate's car not believing in a million years that what the doctor said was correct.

Appendicitis meant surgery and I really didn't think that was going to happen. I was scared when I understood and accepted that they really did need to operate so my body did the thing it always did when it was afraid, it froze. Inside I felt as though I was screaming but on the outside I was human portrait of a still lake. I soldiered on and did whatever they told me to do so that the procedure would be over quickly, and I could go home.

And here I am, I thought lying on a cold steel surgery table, *waiting to be wheeled into surgery.* My mind was still rejecting what was about to happen, but at this point I had been given more medication and world felt like cotton candy. Noises would bounce gently around me, and everything felt like it was in slow motion. I was naked except for the hospital gown and felt the cold metal table against my body as my head rested on the small square hospital pillow. My head and eyelids felt like they had weights attached to them and I could barely keep them open. I suddenly felt nauseous and dizzy as though I was going to throw up but instead I turned my head to the side and closed my eyes. I open them when I feel someone touch my calf and see that I had been wheeled into the surgical room. I squint at the bright lights and lift my head, looking towards my leg to watch a nurse place some sort of square rectangular sticker on my calf. She looked up at me when I asked what it was. "It's to ensure that you ground any electric current during surgery," she said. *What is she talking about?* I thought. The world was moving in slow motion and my brain and voice seemed too far in my body to reach and use. Before I had a chance to ask her what she meant by that, another nurse told me to count backwards from ten. I think I got to eight before I blacked out.

My eyes open and I see two doctors standing up slightly leaning over me. One of them looks over at me and frantically looks behind me. I hear a noise and I black out again.

I become conscious when the nurses transfer me from the surgery table to the gurney and yelp in agony as they both use the four corners of the sheet to launch me onto the bed. The pain was excruciating. My lower abdomen felt like someone just stabbed me with a double-edged knife and used it to core out the appendage. Everything went black again after that.

The next time I wake it's dark and I'm in a room with a desk off to one side. My cousin is sleeping on a chair nearby. She hears me stir and asks if I'm okay. I tell her yes and as soon as I do, I am overcome with an uncontrollable urge to urinate. I try to sit up but can barely move because of the pain from surgery. I am groggy and my head feels like a twenty-pound bowling ball. I sit back and my cousin helps me with the bedpan. I am lying down looking up at her and she's telling me I need to urinate into the bedpan. For the life of me, I could not execute the task. I found it impossible to stay conscious for long enough and my body was simply not cooperating. My cousin helped me sit up despite the agony in doing so, and held me there until I was able to go. I kept falling in and out of sleep and each time I did my body would sway slightly and I'd be woken up by the blinding pain on my lower right side. The nurses kept coming in asking my cousin if I had gone yet. "Not yet," she responded smiling.

"Can we talk to you for a minute?" a nurse asks. My cousin leaves and comes back a minute later and sits beside me.

"They want to insert a catheter," Anna says in Italian.

"What is that?" I ask her.

"It's a tube connected to your bladder to drain the urine." We both look at each other and know that there is no way I'll be able to handle that type of invasion so in a semi-conscious state of emergency, but trying also to concentrate and calm down so that I could go, my cousin and I both celebrated an hour later when I finally relieved myself.

A few hours later I wake again to see Luca coming through the door with flowers. I'm still in the same room and in the light of day see that my bed is against the wall in a room with no other patients. There is a desk on the other side, and it looks like I'm in an office. Across the hall I see the same size room, but with four patients in each corner. I'm told I will be transferred to that room once a space frees up. I ask hospital staff if there is a phone anywhere to make a collect call and they tell me they have a phone on a rolling dolly that they can bring over when I need it. Luca and I talk about the surgery and what I remember of it. "I didn't sleep the entire night," he tells me. "I knew you were going to be okay, but I was so worried." I smile at him and tell him I'm glad it's over. He stays for the weekend in Florence and hangs out in the hospital with me keeping me company and helping me through my day. Within twenty-four hours I was up and walking the corridors of the wing. I wanted to go home as soon as possible and was trying to make that happen in any way I could.

"Rosamaria Sangiorgio e al telefono. Acetti la telefonata?" I hear my mother's voice muffled on the phone answer, "No." when she's asked to accept the collect call.

"Ma, it's me." I try to speak over the operator, but she interrupts and asks my mother again.

"Rosamaria Sangiorgio e al telfono. Accetti la telefonata?"

"No," I hear my mother say. "Non acetto."

I hear the phone disconnect and then the sound of the operator's voice telling me that the call was not accepted. "Okay. Thank you." I respond feeling stupid. I turn slowly making sure the drips I was attached to do not tangle or get caught on anything. I shuffle back slowly to my bed and lie down. I don't understand why my mother didn't accept my collect call. What had I done this time? My mind searches for the answers but the only thing I pull from my repertoire was how much of a failure I was and no wonder she didn't speak to me.

I'm still in the hospital a few days later but this time with my cousin. I hadn't seen her since the surgery, and we sat chatting about different things including my anticipated release date. I developed a fever after the surgery and was told it was due to an infection inside one of my fallopian tubes.

"I'm glad they didn't remove it while you were in surgery."

"What?" I respond.

"Well, your appendix became inflamed because of the infection in your fallopian tube. They wanted to remove the one tube completely, but I told them they needed to treat the infection with antibiotics before removing it," Anna explained. "It's amazing you weren't in more pain considering what was going on." I was dumbfounded. "Who in their right mind thinks to remove a fallopian tube just like that?" I ask incredulously. "I agree," she responded. "And if they could treat it with antibiotics then they should do that first rather than figuring first to remove a reproductive organ." I shook my head. I could not believe what I was hearing. While I was not in control of my body, someone was going to remove and manipulate an organ that I needed to bear children. Instantly upon that realization a feeling of fear washed over me. I could not trust anyone. Not my parents, not my family and now, not even medical professionals. It was as if fear wrapped itself around my throat and gave it a tight squeeze. I shivered and tried again to focus on what my cousin was saying but it was impossible. My body reacted to the feeling of my safety being compromised so it becomes harder to breath air into my lungs. It becomes harder to breathe, so I start to breathe faster. *Will she notice? No. She can't notice. Concentrate! Concentrate! Concentrate!* I tell myself.

"I didn't call your parents when you went into the hospital, I called Aunt Giulia instead since we were in the same time zone," she went on, "I told her you were in surgery and let her know it was appendicitis. She asked if the diagnosis of appendicitis was real or if I was lying and you had gotten pregnant. It was infuriating. Thankfully, my boyfriend's mother took the phone out of my hand and gave her a piece of her mind."

"What did she say?" I asked.

"She told her that this was not a question to ask since we are two young girls dealing with a situation requiring adult guidance. The question of whether or not Rosemary is lying should not even come to mind. Rosemary is in the hospital and had surgery to remove her appendix and her family is thousands of miles away. That should be the only thing that is important right now."

I could not believe my ears. Again, this ridiculous obsession with my sexual behavior and then questioning whether the appendicitis was just a cover. "And what did it matter?" I said to Anna. "Exactly!" she responded.

I felt sick. How could my family be so brutal to think I was lying about the surgery? What lie did I ever tell them to make them think this way? I mean sure I had lied here and there about where I was going when I lived at home, but I would never lie about something like this. I was in the hospital, post-surgery in a foreign country and their concern was making sure that their support was being given for the right reasons. It was nauseating to even fathom the thought. I despised my family and was grateful I was far away despite where I was in that moment.

"And" continued Anna. "Guess which doctor spoke to your mother after the surgery?" I shrug my shoulders. "The one that wanted to remove the fallopian tube. He told your mother that the reason you had appendicitis in the first place was because you were on the pill which is what caused the infection in your fallopian tube. The other doctor didn't agree with him at all and told me that it was most likely an infection that was never treated and for some reason you weren't feeling the pain from it. But of course, he's not the doctor that spoke to your mother."

"Of course!" I respond to my cousin.

Unreal, I thought. *No wonder she didn't accept the call. She thinks I had surgery for some other reason.* I am heartbroken putting the pieces together of my family's perception of me. *What does it matter anyway if I was pregnant or not? It's not like anyone did a good job in protecting me anyway.* I shake my head in silent disbelief, letting this tragedy sink in. *How does this keep getting worse? How could they think I would lie about surgery? Why don't they believe anything about me? What did I do to earn their distrust?* I search my mind and cannot understand. *Who is this person they think I am? Why do I keep having to defend myself when I've done nothing wrong?* I wished I had died somehow in surgery just so that I didn't have to wake up in the reality I was living in. I went home a week later with an even greater feeling of solitude. I understood, very deep in my psyche, that I was on my own, so I stopped looking for approval from my parents and concentrated solely on building a happier life without them.

FIVE

RUNNING SCARED

"Rose! Rose! Wake up! Rose!" I hear Luca's voice getting louder.

"What's your name?! How old are you?!" I hear a stranger's voice.

"Rose," I say softly, "twenty." I open my eyes and see Luca's face looking down at me.

"Where are we?" I say weakly.

"We are at the café," he responds, "you fainted."

"What did you say?" I ask then realize I am lying on the ground. I try to sit up and my head is heavy. "Slowly, slowly," Luca says helping me. I look around and see that I'm in the café down the street from Luca's house. I don't remember anything after walking into the café.

"How long was I out?" I ask him. "A few minutes," he responds. Someone working at the café appears next to me and hands me a glass of water. I take it and drink slowly trying to put my thoughts together. *Fainted? Shit. Well, that's never happened before.* I knew I was sleep deprived, stressed and a bit shaky, but I had never fainted before because of my anxiety symptoms and any event, *it's not like*

*those symptoms don't exist every day for me. So, what was
the issue now?* I thought. Every panic episode I ever had up
to that point I had *felt* that I was going to pass out, but never
did. *But I wasn't having an attack.* I thought. This was new
for me. As I sit there gathering my thoughts I hear Chum-
bawamba's 'Tubthumping' playing in the background. *How
appropriate* I think.

It had been a little over a year since the surgery and in
that time I went to Canada to complete my high school
diploma. I choose a school in another district so that I could
keep my distance between my parents and I and it worked
out well. I completed my high school diploma and then left
for Italy again to enroll myself into the University of
Florence for a degree in Foreign Language and Literature. I
wasn't excited to go back to Italy and leave my friends again,
but it was the decision I had made and the decision I was
sticking to. I never wanted to live with my parents ever
again.

I slowly stand with Luca's help and take a seat at one of
the café tables. I am handed another glass of water but this
one I'm told is with sugar. I take a sip and feel the sugar
crystals in the water, and it feels like I'm drinking sweet-
ened sand. On the outside I appear calm and steady, but on
the inside, I am utterly and hopelessly terrified. I'm shocked
that I fainted and take sips of water while I survey my
surroundings to take note of where everyone is in the café
and my fastest exit in case I need to leave. I am scared but
don't know why. There is nothing to fear in front of me and
the people in the café have been kind, yet I'm still feeling
terribly afraid as though someone might walk through the
front door with a weapon, and I cannot shake this feeling of
fear. I'm afraid of something but it's not clear what it is.

I cannot make sense of it, so I look around the café

attempting to do so. I notice there are no women in the bar in the café and a few men standing by the espresso machine drinking coffee. I lower my eyes so that I don't have to meet theirs. I stare intently at the water in the cup that I'm drinking. Suddenly, I feel Lyle's hand on my back. He is nowhere near me, but I feel his hand on my back. I physically move my shoulders and arms to get his imaginary hands off me. Luca is staring at me concerned but I'm pretending not to notice and instead turn to look outside wondering when I'll be able to escape so that I can be alone.

"I'm okay," I reassure him still looking outside at the accumulating morning traffic. "I'm probably just exhausted and need sleep. I'm going to head home." *Which was the plan in the first place until you followed me here.* I think to myself. I look at him and can tell by his eyes that I've wounded him. "Why don't you want to come back to my place?" he asks. I squint and turn my head slightly to look at him. *Because the last place I want to be is with you in your apartment. Didn't we have the same night of arguing where all you did was accuse me of cheating on you? For no reason at all?* Luca looks back at me as though I had said the words aloud. I look into his eyes and instead say, "I just want to go home." He nods in understanding, and I feel him take a softer line towards me. "I'll accompany you on the bus but then I'll have to come back home." I nod silently, feeling relieved. I can't wait to get home where I am safe.

The university program I enrolled in was technically four years, but most students finished in five. I was doing well so far, most times obtaining higher marks on my exams than my Italian counterparts. I made some friends in my faculty and together we would hang out at a small bar near Piazza Santa Maria Novella. There was a small cover fee to enter the bar, but if you paid an annual membership fee, you could go in and out as you pleased. Bar Otto was where we congregated most weeknights and sometimes used the place on the weekends to meet before heading out as a group. There was a foosball table, and we'd have tournaments against each other if we didn't have anything better to do that night.

A friend in our group, Benedetto (Ben for short), lived in an apartment on the same street as Otto's. He had a bright personality and lived alone in a bachelor pad with a pet mouse for company. He would generally keep the mouse at home in a cage but sometimes he would bring him out using a little drawstring pouch to carry him. The pouch could be worn around your neck and Ben would pin the pouch to whatever shirt he was wearing so that the mouse wouldn't bounce around too much while walking. When Ben would feed him, you'd see the mouse's head pop out of the pouch and stretch his little arms to take food from Ben's fingers. It was an adorable thing to watch.

The night before I fainted, I was in the city already eating dinner with Luca. Afterwards, the plan was to meet everyone at Otto's before heading out again. It was a good night and I felt excited to meet up with my friends since I was looking forward to them meeting Luca. Once we arrived, I saw Ben carrying his pet mouse and as usual, asked if I could hold him. "Of course!" Ben said as he placed the pouch around my neck. I looked down to see the pouch slightly open so I rested my index finger on the edge hoping the mouse would poke his head out. Sure enough, two little black eyes and a set of whiskers emerged to investigate my finger. I watched the mouse's face twitching this way and that, mesmerized by the little creature. I turn back into the conversation when I hear Ben say, "I need to put him in his cage. Come up with me so you can see my apartment." I look over at Luca and he stands there not saying a word. "Come on, let's go," I say to Luca. He shakes his head no, and tells me to go ahead while he pulls a pack of cigarettes from his jacket. I look at him confused and he says, "Go, it's fine." I shrug and head up to the apartment with Ben.

A few minutes later I return downstairs and walk over to Luca. It is dark and as I approach him I can see he is glaring at me. "Did you like seeing his apartment? What took you so long? It's a *bachelor pad.*"

I look back at him confused knowing I was upstairs for less than five minutes.

"Why didn't you come up with us?" I ask.

"Did you like it? You did, didn't you? Of course you liked it," he hisses. I freeze remembering a rendition of those words in my past. I hear the words again in my head but this time they come from Lyle, and I suddenly feel his hand on my back again. *Fuck! What the fuck! What is happening?* I start to shake, and I notice my breathing becoming difficult. I can't get enough air into my lungs. *Not now, not now, not now,* I tell myself hoping that I can somehow stave off my anxiety. I look down and close my eyes and then take a second to move my shoulders around to shake the feeling off. I open my eyes to the reality in front of me as I hear Luca explaining why I had done the ultimate betrayal by going into Ben's apartment.

I roll my eyes and shake my head. *Here we go again,* I thought. Another fight. For some reason, since starting university, Luca had become increasingly more possessive despite the fact I had done nothing to earn his mistrust. It was beginning to feel as though I was not in control of my own choices, which was the last thing I needed. The group we were with walked ahead and the louder Luca and I became, the further they walked away from us. "Great," I say to him. "I guess I can kiss those friends' goodbye on Monday. Do you realize how ridiculous you're acting right now?" We keep arguing and don't notice two policemen walking in our direction until they are beside us. "Can you keep your voices down?" one of them says. "Yes of course," we mumble. We head back to Luca's apartment and the arguing continued there for another few hours while a few neighbors knocked on the door to tell us to keep it down. I didn't sleep the entire night and left for café early the next morning in an attempt to escape and go home. Instead, Luca followed me, and it was there that I collapsed.

A few days after fainting, nightmares of watching my own sexual assault by faceless strangers became a regular nightly occurrence. I hadn't had nightmares like this for about a year but there they were again. I would wake up screaming, sometimes biting my arms or kicking my legs trying to get the stranger off me. I would feel the bed I was sleeping on move as if Lyle was sitting on it again. I had dreams of his hand on my back holding me down while I struggled to breathe and remove myself from his grasp. In my dreams Lyle would always get what he wanted, and I'd wake up feeling ashamed and dirty.

Slowly but surely my body was beginning to feel constricted and tense, but I carried on. During the day I was jittery and restless despite being exhausted from the nightmares. I was tired but afraid to close my eyes. The scenes from my mind would conjure up in my nightmares somehow and eventually became an impending reality in my waking hours. I became convinced that I was not safe if I went out because if I had another episode that caused me to faint, it would be inevitable that someone would take advantage of me while I was unconscious. As absolutely strange and illogical as it sounds, this was my conviction. I felt it in my bones. These thoughts were on repeat in my brain and I became fearful of the world and what would happen to me if I lost control.

Within three weeks of fainting at the cafe, my chronic anxiety and panic disorder morphed into full-blown agoraphobia, except I didn't know what was wrong with me. I did not have access to any information or any person that could educate me about anxiety, trauma or mental illness. All I could understand was that I was afraid and the more I feared, the smaller my world became. My anxiety symptoms became so unbearable that it was easier to just stay home. I began with avoiding lineups, busses, classrooms and stores. Eventually, I was not going anywhere alone. Period. I fell behind in my classes and loathed myself for it. I had this incredible opportunity of being able to attend university in a beautiful city, but couldn't do anything with it. I hated myself. I hated everything about myself. I hated that my family was right about me and that yes, something *was* wrong with me. Each day I woke up I wished I didn't. I was angry that I had been born and felt I didn't deserve to live because it was obvious to me that I was defective.

When I didn't think it could get any worse, I began having issues at home. It began with dizziness and then eventually I felt so dizzy that to make it to the bathroom was a struggle. Lying down in my bed caused the same dizziness however to a lesser extent, so my bed became my island and my apartment was the lava. I could not do much of anything if I was alone in my apartment. I thought I would trip and fall, choke on something or faint while alone at home which would then cause paramedics to rescue me and then it was back to the hospital where the doctors would do atrocious things to me. Eventually I became mostly confined to my bed and my room, only traveling around to the kitchen or bathroom and common areas when necessary making my way by leaning on walls, chairs or doorframes to help stop my head from spinning. I stopped eating, showering and sleeping when I was home alone. All the stress associated from doing any of those things became too much for me and would send me into a panic, so I stopped. The intrusive thoughts were on a repetitive loop in my head, and I could not stop them. What if I had an accident and lost consciousness? What if I started choking and lost consciousness? What if I slipped in the shower and lost consciousness? Who would find me? What would they do to me? I stopped heading to the mailbox three flights down the stairs to the ground floor. There wasn't a chance I would risk three flights of stairs if my roommate could easily pick up the mail. What if I fell? And then what? It all seemed so logical to me that any of these illogical scenarios were certainties that would occur. For me it was as clear as the sun and moon in the sky.

Oddly enough, a psychiatrist worked out of the unit below mine. He was a mere twelve steps away from my apartment, but I could not bring myself to contact him. What if I was sent away to a hospital? What if I became confined or detained in some way? The thought of being restrained inside a hospital was something I was certain would happen if I shared what I was experiencing with someone else. I believed I'd had some sort of psychosis or psychotic break and that the person who I was had disappeared. Many days I would sit in the entry way of my apartment with the front door wide open observing the stairwell landing. I would listen for any sign of life going in or out of the apartment below yet each time I would hear activity, I could never muster the courage to call out for help. I lived in this world of terror for six months having absolutely no idea at all what was wrong with me.

On February 23, 1997, I wrote in my journal that *'I feel sick. I feel dead. I'm scared to go out. I'm scared to stay alone. I don't feel myself. When I talk I feel the words coming from someone else. I feel things aren't happening to me, that they're happening to another person. I don't understand what I'm saying when I speak. I seem to think I say things that I don't hear. I am paranoid that people are looking at me like I'm a freak or that I'm crazy.'*

A few weeks later, on April 15th I wrote, *'Last night I woke up convinced I was going to go mental and kill myself without knowing. Could that even be possible?'*

My agoraphobic state was by far the most terrifying period of my life. I didn't understand I had a mental disorder because I didn't trust anyone enough to tell them what was going on in my head. Luca understood I wasn't well but since I was somewhat normal in his presence, he couldn't see the other side of it. He was my safe person and when I was with him I was able to work through any symptoms I was having.

I hear the shrill of the phone ring in the other room. I get up from bed and walk into the kitchen to pick it up. 'Pronto?'

"Hi, Ro! How are you?!" I hear and recognize my cousin's voice and smile. "I'm good Dmitri, how about you?" I ask. I sit down on a nearby chair and settle into it knowing this may be a long call. We start the call on a great note, discussing what we are both doing in school.

"Yea. Spanish class is great!" I say to him. "It's confusing sometimes since it's so similar to Italian, but I'm managing." I chatter about things I did the year before in university since he wouldn't know the difference. I am lying easily, loathing myself while I'm hearing myself speak. I haven't been to a class in months. As I am talking I feel my throat. I feel every movement my body is making inside to utter the words I am saying. *What is wrong with the vibrations in your vocal chords?* The intrusive thought come out of nowhere. *There is something wrong, something is happening. What is happening? Why do the vibrations in my throat feel that way? Is that normal? What is that noise? Is that my voice? What is wrong with my voice? Is someone else in the apartment with me?*

"What about you?" I ask him as my panic intensifies. "What have you been up to?" I cover the phone receiver with one hand and try to control my breathing, but I can't.

Why does the voice on the phone sound weird? Why is the voice sounding unsteady? What are those noises? Is that a person on the other end of this phone? Why does everything sound so broken? Who is this person on the other side of the phone? What was he talking about? Why can't I remember the last few minutes? How did I get on this phone call? Slowly but surely I enter a state of panic.

"Hey, Dmitri, I need to get going," I blurt out.

"Uh, sure." He responds a little taken aback by my sudden interruption.

"Sorry, I just remembered I need to be somewhere in an hour." I lie again. "Call me on Tuesday and we can pick up the conversation where we left off."

"Sure. Okay, no problem. Hey listen. Are you okay?" he asks. *No, I'm not okay. I'm failing all my classes, I'm barely eating, hardly sleeping. I'm scared to live, and I'm scared to die. I hate myself and my family doesn't want anything to do with me. I'm sick of being alone but I can't tolerate anyone close to me either.* "Yes of course," I answer. "I just didn't realize the time."

"Okay, but it's not that." Dmitri presses on.

"I'm fine. Honestly. Everything is great. I need to get going though."

"Okay. Call me soon," Dmitri says.

I hang up the phone and look around. I am alone in the apartment, and it is quiet. I sit on my bed and try to make sense of what just happened, but I had no idea. The light is on in my room, so I turn it off and return to my bed while turning on my small desk lamp. I sit in bed and remain fixated the whole night trying to figure out what happened and having absolutely no idea on how I am going to navigate being scared of my voice and of voices on the phone. *How did I get here?* I think to myself. As hard as I try I cannot find any pattern leading me to a place in my life where I was almost afraid to breathe.

I awake the next morning in a haze and open my eyes instantly feeling dizzy. I close them again and wait a few minutes before reattempting. I managed to sleep for a few hours once the sun started coming up and then lay in bed staring at sun beams as they moved across the wall. I take a deep breath and sit up, turning the switch to my desk lamp off in the light of day. It had been months since I slept in a darkened room. I woke up too many times shaking and screaming from nightmares and then waking up to the darkness would scare me even more. Sleeping with the light on was helpful as it made me less afraid to fall asleep.

How am I going to fix this? I wondered to myself. I got up and headed to the bathroom avoiding my reflection. I haven't looked into a mirror in over six months because the last time I did, the person staring back at me appeared distorted and I had a severe anxiety attack because of it. I squeeze toothpaste on my toothbrush and begin to brush my teeth. I want to look in the mirror but am afraid I won't recognize the girl in the mirror. *Of what? What are you afraid of? This is not you, remember?* I felt a voice come from deep within. Unlike the intrusive voice, this voice soothed me. I spit out the water and toothpaste and wiped my face with a towel. *Remember? Do you remember?* I rest my hands on either side of the sink and take a deep breath in and out. *What am I afraid of? Remember? Do you remember? What do you remember? Who are you? Do you remember? Do you remember who you are?* I look at my knuckles, and notice they are white from gripping the sides of the sink. I lift my head and look into the mirror. My hair is messy, and my skin is pale. My dark brown eyes are bloodshot, and my eyelids are a bright fleshy pink. *Do you remember who that is?* I place one of my hands on the mirror beside my face.

"This is not me. I am not like this. This is not who I am. This is not who you are," I say out loud startling myself. My voice sounds clear and steady. I pause and look into my own eyes and keep going. "This is not you. This is not who you are." I feel the vibrations of my vocal cords and feel the fear rising up in my throat. I push the thought away. *It's okay,* I say to myself. *Keep going.* Again, out loud, "This is not who you are. This is not who you will be." I say while staring at my reflection in the mirror. I keep my hand on the mirror and repeat the phrases a few more times until I'm comfortable enough to head back to bed. *That's enough for today,* I think. I feel as though something has changed, but I'm not sure what.

SIX

LA NAUSÉE

I decide to ask my parents if I could come home in early summer so that I could spend time with my friends for a few weeks before heading back to school. I didn't know how I was going to get there since I couldn't exit my front door alone, but I decided to worry about that later. I was hoping that by being in a familiar place, I would magically turn back into the old me, just as I had magically turned into this person I couldn't recognize. It was the only solution I could come up with. My parents were excited that I wanted to come home and "because I was so busy at school" I asked if they could purchase the plane ticket and leave it at the check-in counter at the airport. They agreed and a few weeks later, I left for Canada accompanied by a carry-on, my cassette player and headphones, and a plethora of extra strength nausea pills to keep me cocooned within my own reality. It had become habit for me to use pills regularly to function. It had started the year before and was mainly centered around things I could take to stay awake and things I could take to sleep. Marijuana kept me hungry, so I rationalized that all the bases were covered for me to keep living healthily. Little did I know this habit was one I would carry into my adult life.

When I arrive at the airport in Rome there is an older woman standing in front of me at the ticket counter having issues with the agent. I line up a few feet behind her and stand to wait but begin immediately hyperventilating. Lines were particularly awful to stand in at the height of my agoraphobia despite the pills I had taken. I start to panic and decide to jump in as a translator to hurry the conversation along as I hear both English and Italian in front of me. I walk up to the counter and tell them I'm bilingual. The agent looks at me relieved and explains the issue. The woman has a reserved ticket and to retrieve it, he will need payment. I turn to the woman and begin explaining in English what she is not understanding in Italian. As I am speaking to her the woman turns to me and slurs, "What're you doing here?"

I stop talking and turn my head the other way so that I don't have to breathe in the smell of alcohol that seems to be emanating from every pore in her body. She is inebriated and angry and all I want to do is get onto that plane, swallow a few more anti-nauseants and wake up in Canada. She was now in the way of that, and my anxiety begins to swell. *No. No. No.* I scream wildly to myself. *Please no,* I begged myself. *Not here. I can't pass out here.* The anti-nausea has made me drowsy, so my anxiety felt like it was enclosed in a box, trying to get out. I speak louder and repeat that to pick up the plane ticket, the agent needs payment.

She turns her entire body directly to face me and leans on the counter. I look down as something falls to the floor from her flayed open fanny pack and reach to pick it up. I realize a few $100 bills are on the ground, so I pick them up and hand them to her with both hands as though I'm presenting them. She snatches them from my hands and crumples them back into her pack. I can see that there are at least 50 or more $100 dollar bills, so I warn her to zip the pack. "Who cares!" she says loudly. "My kids, my kids did this. I can't believe my kids did this to me," she rambles on almost incoherently. "Do you want to know what happened to me? My kids. My kids and I had lunch and the next thing I know is I'm here at the airport. They paid for a cab that dropped me off here and stuffed this thing full of money. Can you believe it? They don't want me around."

I stare back at her as I certainly *can* believe it. Every word she utters I am overwhelmed by the smell of drink on her breath. I spend a few minutes speaking back and forth with the agent until the ticket is figured out. I'm concentrating on moving her along but suddenly there is a sharp pain in my stomach. I need to sit down but I keep pushing forward. *I need to get out of this situation as soon as possible,* I say to myself. The woman finally leaves the counter with her ticket, and a few minutes later I have my own ticket as well. I thank the agent and head to the gate but not without noticing the lady's carry-on that she left randomly near the ticket counter. I sigh and take my bag as well as hers to the security line and hand her the bag. She is talking to someone else about how her children are animals for leaving her at the airport with ticket money. I wonder about her children, who they are and what they may have had to endure. I hand her the bag and she recognizes me, but I move out of the situation quickly, telling her I need to catch another plane when in reality, we are on the same flight. As I wait for the aircraft to board, I move around the terminal, so she doesn't notice me or call me over. Moving around keeps me calm and my headphones provided the additional buffer between the world and me. As I'm turning a corner, I see that there is somewhere I can sit, away from people but also in sight of the entry gate to the plane. I wait until my seat rows are called and once aboard, I buckle myself in and close my eyes. *I made it,* I congratulate myself. I reach down into my pack and take a few anti-nauseants before the plane takes off. I am utterly exhausted and do not have the energy to read one page of the book nestled in my bag.

A few hours later I wake up groggy and leave my seat to use the bathroom. As I head to the back of the plane, I see the lady slumped over her seat, sleeping alone in the middle of a 5-seat row. I watch her as I walk by and deduct from the awkward position she is in, that her body will not be forgiving when she wakes up. "She's had too much to drink. I'm glad she's asleep," a stewardess says to me as she passes and sees me looking at her. I am glad too but for other reasons, one of them being that we were landing soon, and the other, that maybe I would return to normal in the next few days. I feel a tinge of excitement for the first time in months.

———

I am startled by a loud knock on my bedroom door. "Yes?" I call out. My mom pops her head inside my room, "Buongiorno! I made an appointment for you at the doctor for the headaches you've been having. We'll be heading out at 2:30."

I look up from my book casually but feel myself trembling already, "I don't need to go anymore. I don't have a headache. Maybe it was just jetlag."

She looks at me and responds, "Let's go anyway because

I've made the appointment. We should go for a quick check-up now that you are here."

"No, it's okay. I'll go another time," I insist. Inside I am screaming, *I can't go! I can't go! Everyone is going to find out!* Nothing had magically changed when I arrived home earlier that month and I was deathly afraid of my family finding out I had something wrong with me.

"No, you're not going another time. I need to pick up a prescription for your father anyway. We are going today," she answers back. "You've been here for a week, and you have not stepped foot outside. You need some fresh air too, so we are going." I sigh and roll my eyes at her. "Fine," I say knowing that I will not win. She closes my bedroom door and I sit there staring out of the window wishing I could disappear. I know I can't get out of this one.

She is not completely correct with her observations about me though, I thought. *I've been home for two weeks and went to Lauriana's for dinner.* As soon as the thought enters my mind I know it makes no difference anyway considering how quickly I turned around and went back home. I arrived at Lauriana's and within ten minutes I let her know I wasn't feeling well. Since my father didn't have a cell phone and I needed him to pick me up, I had to wait for my father to arrive back home to take my call. As I sat there on Lauriana's couch waiting for my dad to arrive home, I spiraled even further down the anxiety wormhole. *Maybe my friend called to tell my mom how I was acting while I was at her house?* I thought. *Or maybe her mother? Yes. Maybe her mother, that must be it.* The reality was that no one had called my parents but me, and it was for a pick-up. I was paranoid of people talking behind my back since I had grown so accustomed to it in my family.

For the next few hours before going to the doctor, I am

behind closed doors spiraling. *I can't leave. I can't go. What if we get into an accident on the way there? What if I pass out? What if the doctor tells me I need to check-into a hospital? I can't go. I can't leave. I can't go. I can't leave.* My anxiety takes over completely when I hear my mother knock on my bedroom door. "Let's go!" she sings. I open the door. "I'm not going," I say flatly to her face. She looks back at me and immediately understands I'm panicking. She grabs my arm and does not let go while I fight her the entire way to the car. She puts me into the passenger side of the vehicle, buckles my seat belt, and closes the door. I am too afraid to jump out and run back into the house so I sit trapped in the car, staring at the front door trying to will the entire house closer so that I can step out of the car and get back into my room.

Once my mother gets into the driver's seat and turns the ignition on, my anxiety becomes intolerable and takes on a life of its own. For the ten-minute ride to the doctor's office, I have a severe panic episode while my mother is driving. She tries to settle me by caressing my hair and trying to hold my hand, but I am writhing in pain and hyperventilating. Her caressing hand is somehow physically hurting me. We arrive and there are a few other people in the waiting room including the doctor taking a folder from the top of the secretary's desk. At this point I am shaking, crying, and bent over in pain. I am doing my best to be silent, but I am whimpering. My mother helps me to the door and as I walk in everyone turns their head to look at me. Dead silence. I feel like an animal in a cage at a zoo. The doctor looks at my mother and I and gestures for us to go directly into his office. A second later the chatter in the office picks up again. I hear him talking as I'm walking away from him, but I can't focus on anything. I sit in one of his chairs crying silently and shaking so hard in one of his chairs that my teeth are chattering. My mother is sitting next to me silently stroking my hair. It hurts and I move away from her hand so that she stops touching me. I cannot control my energy at all. I don't want anyone touching me. Everything that does feels like it's branding me.

When the doctor comes in, he sits at his desk directly in front of me. I know he's looking at me and wants to talk but I could not regulate my breathing or calm the pain in my body to do so. I am embarrassed by what he and my mother are witnessing and keep my head down trying to regain composure. He waits and sees that I cannot calm down.

Without a word he leaves the room and comes back, injecting me with a needle that I don't see coming. Once he is finished he leaves the room again telling me he'll be right back. After a few minutes, everything starts to slow down, and my breathing does too. I am aware and alert, but my body feels more relaxed. I am tense but am not shaking uncontrollably. The doctor comes back and takes a seat at his desk again. He watches me for a minute and then asks quietly, "What's wrong?"

I feel like a volcano erupting. He has been my doctor for years and I trust him, so I tell him everything. I tell him about my anxiety that never goes away and how it got much worse with the move to Italy. I talk about how hard it is living there, day after day, and feeling alone. "I am never alone," I tell him, "but I feel so detached and isolated." I talk about the nightmares, mental fogginess, confusion and the eerie way I am fearful of my own voice, and voices on the phone. I describe the panic episodes explaining that they come out of nowhere and overtake me. I mention nothing of the abuse I endured or the fear of being raped since I believe it has nothing to do with anything.

"'It's gotten so bad that I haven't left my apartment in six months.

The doctor looks up from his notes.

"What do you mean by that?" he asks.

"I mean exactly that. I mean I haven't left my apartment in six months."

"How did you manage to get onto the flight?"

"I took enough antinauseants that they kept me drowsy."

"What about school?"

"'I didn't go."

"What about groceries?"

"Luca bought them for me."

He is staring at me, and I am staring back at him. I hear my mother sigh beside me. I hate myself. I loathe myself. I am so ashamed. I turn away from his face and wait to hear what will happen and what my consequences will be. I have nothing left to say so I just sit there. The room is silent while he takes notes and I wonder what he's writing. I think that maybe it's something like, "Anxiety turned to psychosis, patient is out of touch with reality. Can't perform daily functions." I feel nothing as I wait for what he will say next.

He looks up while handing me a prescription and tells me to come back in two or three weeks which would be how long the medication would take to start making a difference. I looked at him blankly wondering if he had heard anything I had said in the last twenty minutes. "And don't worry," he added, "the medication I'm giving you will make it easier for you to come here next time." I nodded as he handed me the prescription. He did not diagnose me or discuss what was wrong, but from his response I felt relieved his first reaction was not to put me into a straitjacket. I left quickly in case he changed his mind.

The next morning I hear my parents' hushed voices coming from the kitchen. "But I don't understand," my father was asking my mother, "why didn't she go to school?"

"Because she was scared. Her anxiety is stopping her. I don't know." I hear my mother say. I grab a pillow and put it over my head so I can't hear them talking about me. *I couldn't do it. I just couldn't go places.* I wish I could explain it to them. About how impossible it was for me to even step onto the threshold of my 4th floor apartment. My father leaves for the day and I hear my mother walk up the stairs & gently open my bedroom door. I'm turned the other way so she can't see my face, but I close my eyes anyway and wish her away. I hear the door close softly and feel ashamed that I have failed so miserably at keeping myself together. No wonder they don't want me around. All I am, is a worthless burden.

A few days later my father arrives home with a plastic binder that encases a workbook and cassette tapes. He calls me down from my room to tell me that a friend of his was having a bit of the same troubles I was. His symptoms were not as severe, but my dad presented the information as something that could perhaps help me. "Why don't you take the first tape and give it a listen?" my dad suggests, "If you're not interested just let me know and maybe we can find something else to help you."

I take a deep breath and say okay while taking the first cassette out of its compartment. I figured the only way to make me get back to who I was required extensive, if not permanent, hospitalization. "Thanks, Dad," I say climbing the stairs. I feel his eyes watching me and my heart floods with guilt. I know he is trying to help, but I am broken and there is nothing that he could do to fix me. No wonder he and my mother didn't like me. I was a constant weight on their shoulders. I pop the cassette into the player and for the first few minutes, I listen to how the program works. Once the initial instructions are over, I hear a woman's voice that introduces herself as Lucinda Bassett. She begins speaking about her childhood and the feelings she had when she was little girl describing that she felt different and apart from everyone else. I become more interested in what she was saying as I felt the same way she did when I was small. After about ten minutes I begin to cry as I hear her describe the mental and physical symptoms that I was having for the past six months. The feelings of disassociation, dizziness, ongoing nightmares, panic, the body pains, being house-bound and the constant feeling of dread, were symptoms normal for the illness defined as agoraphobia.

There it was. The word that set me free. If the condition had a name then it wasn't as irregular as I thought. The mere knowledge that my condition had a name, lifted a weight off my shoulders that enabled me to place myself on the road to healing.

My world sprung open like a jack-in-the box with the understanding that I had a mental illness that was treatable and that there was a way out of the hell I had been living in. I cried with joy and ran downstairs to tell my dad I'd like a copy of the program.

SEVEN

HOMECOMING

The cassette tapes were a 15-week cognitive behavioral therapy (CBT) self-help program that taught coping skills and methods to harness one's ability to control their body's responses to stressors in their everyday environment. I had no idea that coping skills even existed to deal with my symptoms and each skill I learned was like a magical key that helped open a door that my agoraphobia and anxiety had closed. Each day that passed I learned skills to harness my fears and practiced them at all times, in every waking conscious moment. It was hard work, but I believed in small victories as huge milestones which helped my self-esteem along. I slowly learned to love myself and take care of myself again.

At that time, I did not delve into why I had specific stressors, for example facing the reality of where my fear of rape was from. Since Lyle hadn't raped me, but only attempted to a few times, I would rationalize and attach the symptoms of stress I was feeling to current events like the fact that I was far from home, or that I didn't sleep well the night before. In my mind I had agoraphobia triggered by panic disorder and my logic did not take the issue any further. I did not think about the impact of the trauma I endured, or the trauma I was enduring by being the scape-goat in my family and by being gaslit to believe what Lyle had done to me was not a big deal. I dismissed the impact of continuously wearing a mask among all the members in my family, year after year. I had suppressed the sexual abuse so successfully that I believed whatever mental challenges I was dealing with were a direct result of my *own* shortcom-ings. I felt that something was wrong with *me* and that I was born with a brain that didn't work properly. I believed I was ill equipped to lead a mentally healthy life and that some-thing had gone wrong during my in-utero development. I knew my mother had a difficult pregnancy and childbirth with me and I slotted this in my mental back-pocket as well. I wanted to have children but didn't want to risk the chance of passing along whatever illness I had to them. I dismissed the abuse and trauma as having anything to do with my mental condition and blamed myself for everything that was happening. I believed I was the problem and the trauma had absolutely nothing to do with it. The way my family treated me reinforced these beliefs.

Besides this elephant-sized 'blind spot,' I began by reviewing chapter one, setting aside two weeks to read, study and put into practice the coping skills I was learning. I worked each and every waking moment to tame the fear. Before attempting any of the exposure exercises like going to the grocery store or taking the bus by myself, I worked on understanding what agoraphobia was and how hormones like cortisol, and neurotransmitters like serotonin worked. My diet changed overnight. I drastically cut out caffeine and began paying more attention to the foods I was consuming and the times I was consuming them at. The medication I was prescribed helped with sleeping and gave my body the time to rest and recoup so that I was able to work on the skills I was learning. My symptoms scared me and kept me locked in a state of fear. I thought it would be impossible to do what the program told me to do, which was pay attention to my symptoms so that I could control them. This seemed like the exact opposite of what I had been doing my whole life up to that point. Instead of feeling symptoms and ignoring them until they 'went away,' I now needed to pay attention to them. If the symptom wasn't communicating anything important or helpful, I would begin an internal dialogue with myself to work on changing how I was feeling. My inner dialogue usually resembled something like, *'Why do I feel dizzy? Well, I'm on a bus and I haven't done that in a long time. I've done it before, but lately I've convinced myself that I am not safe, but I am. I need to take deep breaths and repeat 'I am safe' until I feel it.'* I didn't believe any of it at first. I didn't believe that changing the way you speak to yourself can change how you feel but it absolutely did. As I learnt about agoraphobia, I also understood that some symptoms that I thought were the end of me, like the feelings of disassociation, were quite normal under the circumstances. Odd as it may sound, it made me feel less anxious that my body and mind were responding 'normally' as per the illness.

At the start of the CBT, my symptoms were intense. I remember stepping down the front steps of my parents' home and standing on the walkway for thirty-eight seconds (I would time myself) before hurrying inside with my legs shaking and hyperventilating. I continued to soldier on though, and helped myself along to feel safer now that I knew I had an illness I could overcome. A lot of the time I found it impossible to concentrate when I was aiming to complete exposure exercises. On those days I would read an excerpt from the Dhammapada (Buddhist scripture) and concentrate on a saying until I felt myself calm down. Some phrases that stuck with me were, 'An enemy can hurt an enemy, and a man who hates can harm another man; but a man's own mind, if wrongly directed can do him far greater harm,' and also, 'What we are today, come from our thoughts of yesterday, and our present thoughts build our life of tomorrow; our life is creation of our mind.' Choosing a phrase and repeating it would help bring me back into the present moment and ground me, helping me stay in the present.

In addition to the small Buddhist book, I also carried a 'cheat sheet' with me that included other phrases I could concentrate on when I would start feeling panicky. These phrases came from the program or ones I made up myself. Concentrating on sentences like 'This is not anxiety, it's excitement' or 'Of course I feel anxious because ...' (and I would fill in the blank with something), carried me from one location to another. The more I practiced, the better I became at developing new phrases in my head to counteract my thoughts and in turn, my symptoms. I would repeat 'Anxiety is anxious energy,' and would instantly calm down since there was no reason for me to fear energy. Little by little I felt my life loosening up from the tight bundle of nerves I was entangled in. Every single moment of the day my energy and focus went into making conscious choices towards recovery. It was exhausting at first but eventually became easier.

When I returned to school in Florence, Luca helped the first few weeks by following me around on his scooter while I travelled on the bus to class. He would remain in my line of vision for the duration of the ride but one day he challenged me by being out of sight. When he did this I panicked, and my throat immediately closed yet when he reappeared and winked at me I realized he had done it to help me. Eventually I became more comfortable with bus rides after about a month of exposure and Luca helping me along. Of course, some things were easier to do than others for example, showering while alone in the apartment was less scary than eating alone in the apartment but took the same amount of time (about three weeks each) before I felt comfortable doing them alone in my apartment. When I finally went into a supermarket alone and left the store once the clerk cashed me out, I felt I had climbed a mountain. At that point it had been a year since I entered a grocery store by myself, went through the aisles, choose items and patiently made my way through a lineup of customers so that a clerk could cash me out since I needed to overcome each of the smaller activities, to eventually be able to complete the entire activity of a grocery run. My entire life turned into a series of small victories that helped me reach my goals.

I did not have a therapist during this time, so I was on my own with the exposure therapy and controlling my anxiety when it acted up. All I had was the program workbook and the tapes helping me through. I was not successful each time I tried something, and it generally took me two or three tries before I could get through an activity successfully. One of the most useful and liberating things I learned was that no one is paying as much attention to you as you are to yourself. I was always so worried about what I may look like while feeling anxious or having a panic episode in public, but I came to understand that no one is really paying attention to you. Others are mostly paying attention to themselves and as I healed, my confidence grew as well.

The medication the doctor prescribed helped by buffering the intensity of my emotions and symptoms so that I had the mental space to think about how to react to my body symptoms before my body and mind took over. Taking the medication did not heal me, I had to change my thoughts and behaviors to heal myself. Day after day and week after week I found myself crawling out of the cavern I was in and the light at the end of the tunnel becoming brighter and brighter. It took roughly two years to feel comfortable again in doing my usual day-to-day activities. My anxiety and panic attacks did not disappear, but I finally was able to recognize and manage some of my symptoms so that agoraphobia was no longer a part of my life.

Recovering from the mental illness was a turning point for me and I remained dedicated to keeping a healthy, body and mind.

The relationship with Luca deteriorated over time and we eventually parted ways. My agoraphobia impacted his life as well and it was a difficult for him to have a relationship with me during my mental illness. I understood this completely and was incredibly grateful to him for the help he gave so willingly, however he grew more and more irritated as my recovery progressed. I started to feel like a burden to him since I would be reminded almost daily that he helped me recover and now it was my turn to follow his lead in our relationship. This meant whatever choices he made for us I was expected to happily agree, no questions asked. He wanted me to cater to him as '*he catered to me*.' What he didn't understand was that I never wanted to be catered to. I was not well and had a mental illness, but he didn't see it that way. I understood he was angry, and he felt pushed aside in the relationship so I was empathetic and compassionate towards his feelings thinking he would eventually defuse but he didn't. As time went on, instead of becoming closer, we grew apart. I felt him like a ball and chain that would never let me forget how much he helped me so the illness I was so proud of overcoming was being thrown in my face as a weapon. I did my best to explain my thoughts, yet we would continuously go back to the drawing board. I tolerated these arguments for about a year before I decided to let it all go. It became the final say in all of our arguments and the final nail on the coffin when I threw in the towel.

At that point, I was so behind in my degree and felt it was an unattainable goal. I spent a few months thinking about changing my faculty or switching to a trade like silversmithing, yet after much contemplation and my relationship with Luca so far gone, I decided to move back to Canada.

A few weeks after my arrival I began working full-time at a bookstore until I could figure out which direction I wanted to go. Despite how heartbroken I felt leaving a life I thought I was going to have in Italy with Luca, I concentrated on the present to create a new path. I reconnected with old friends and spent a year working at the bookstore before returning to school. I felt alone when I lived away and loved being around my friends again. I was intent on protecting my peace and was ruthless with my boundaries, sometimes getting in my own way of experiencing life and letting go since I wasn't very good at balancing. I feared sinking back into the depressive and anxious state I used to be in so the walls I built became a fortress around me, and the masks I continued to wear helped me move forward.

After returning and moving in with my parents again, what was left of our relationship did not mend. Discussions concerning the abuse were far and few between and would only occur with my mother. I did not raise the topic and neither did she, but every so often something would come up and we would speak about it. My mother did not understand why the abuse affected me so deeply and when I would try to explain it to her, I always left the conversation feeling there was no point. She just didn't get it. From time to time during our discussions, I would tell her tidbits of things Lyle said or did but each time we talked about it, her responses or comments left me retraumatized. "What were you wearing when he came up to you in the kitchen?" or, "Do you think there was any other way to interpret his behavior?" I would stare at her dumbfounded and swear to myself that I would never discuss it with her again, but I always ended up somehow in the same cycle of discussing it and feeling awful for days afterwards. There was always a 'but' with my mother or a 'because.' There was never a conversations where I felt she was on the same planet as I was.

Although it seemed like it to my family, I never accepted any sort of rendition that I was exaggerating about the abuse or that it was all in my head. I wore the mask I was given and also knew that what Lyle did was not okay. I understood he had tried to groom me each time he abused me. I know that if I had not escaped him, he would have raped me. I worried frequently about Tamara's children, Jessica and Simon, and wondered if he was abusing them. In one instance my mother let me know that she had spoken with her sister Bianca, that had called my mother after a worrisome call from Tamara. During the call, Tamara expressed her worry that Jessica was acting erratic and out of character, and she wasn't sure how to get a handle on her. Regina contacted me the next day concerned about her niece's behavior as well asking what I thought. I responded that perhaps what was happening was that her father was abusing her and that this was a way of lashing out. Regina was disturbed by the suggestion, but did not discount that Jessica may be suffering abuse at the hands of her father. A few weeks later when Aunt Bianca brought the subject up with Tamara, a nasty argument ensued, and all discussion was extinguished immediately. Tamara kicked her mother out of her house and reminded her that I was unstable.

Slowly but surely, the good feelings I had after overcoming the agoraphobia and moving back home were drifting further and further away from me. I was back in a world that didn't make sense. Where it was okay to maintain the family narrative that there was something wrong with me and that I could never be happy. Where what he did was not a big deal, and I should just get over it already. Where there was something wrong with me and it had nothing to do with what he did to me.

The intrusive thoughts that I would occasionally have, were now everyday thoughts pulling my self-esteem lower and lower. *I'm worthless, that's why I'm being treated this way. My parents think I'm a lost cause. They will never love me for me. I can't have the things other people have because I'm not capable. There is something wrong with me.* I wanted to be someone else. I wanted out of my body and mind, so I began self-harming again and would do things to frequently put me into harm's way. I would drive with my eyes closed and count the seconds until I would hear honking from a nearby car. I would continue to use over the counter medication as food keeping me regulated and functioning. I would swallow an entire bottle of pills and then minutes later purge and cry and beat myself up for not having the courage to extinguish myself. I binged drugs and alcohol and slept in my car when I couldn't make it home.

Somehow, I completed the college program I had enrolled in with honors, earning myself a graduate's certificate. I looked forward to a new chapter in my life, to working in communications and making enough money to support myself. The relationship between my parents, the constant fighting and bickering and the overall tension in the house did not work for my nervous system. I wanted to return back to a state of autonomy and peace and could not do that living with my parents.

A few months after graduating I landed a full-time job in my field that kept me home only about twelve hours a day. I was okay with this despite being exhausted. I would have rather been tired than not have a way of escape. I concentrated on saving money to move out and began buying small household items that I would keep in my closet to prepare for my departure. The resentment I felt towards my parents was never tame and I physically felt better being away from them. Their lack of action regarding the abuse was constantly and consistently part of me. I could not go anywhere or do anything that would help me escape the thought that my parents did not care about me. A few times I travelled to Florida by myself to visit family and perhaps seeking some sort of validation from other family members it happened to, but I was always unsuccessful. Speaking about it with Regina would always leave me with more questions than answers. I described to her several examples of what he had done to me but months later, she would ask again. I would repeat the incidents and she would simply listen. Again and again, she would listen to stories that I was too ashamed to tell my mother, but nothing changed. The narrative that I was blowing things out of proportion and then dismissed as mentally ill was also not something that changed.

"Do you want to pop by my place and check out the mini village I made?" Tamara asks.

"No thanks," I respond. "I don't want to run into anyone," I add gently. She replies back quickly and without hesitation, "Don't worry, Lyle isn't at home, and he won't be home for hours."

Did I just hear her correctly? Why isn't she asking me the obvious? I look to her for answers but she's staring back, gawking at me like a deer in headlights, eyes agape, waiting for my answer. *Is this real right now?* I think. *How is this happening? She knows that her husband tried to force himself on me and our current discussion validates her knowledge but... I don't understand. Is this a trap? Maybe this is a trap, maybe she wants to have a conversation with me.* I stare back at her knowing this would be the first time in over ten years that we would be in a confined space together privately with the ability to engage in an unsupervised conversation.

"Sure," I answer, "let's go if you know for sure that he won't be there."

"He won't be there." She assures me.

"And he won't pop by? What if he comes home?" I ask nervously. "If he comes home can I just run to your car and hide so I don't have to talk to him?"

"Yes, don't worry. I know you don't want to see him," Tamara confirms.

We get into her car a few minutes later and situate ourselves for the ride that will take roughly a half hour according to my cousin. For the first few minutes of driving,

I watch her maneuver past traffic to the freeway. I'm nervous sitting in the car next to her, trying to understand her intentions but decide to wait patiently wondering what this outing is really about.

A short time later I am seeing cars zoom around us while reading the advertising and street signage dotting the landscape. Tamara quickly begins discussing the miniature village she created. She explains what kind of look and mood she was going for, where she purchased her items, how she created height in scenery and the lighting she had carefully planned out. My cousin seemed relaxed and calm beside me, chattering on without a care in the world as if she didn't know her husband touched a twelve-year-old child's breasts and that the child was her cousin, sitting next to her. I, on the other hand, can't think of anything else and can barely concentrate on anything that she is saying. I am somewhere else, in another world, waiting for her to open up.

We arrive to her house, and she leads the way showing me the storybook themed miniature village she created that had given her some local media attention. The village was massive and took up an entire section of her living room. It was sprawling and intricately detailed in some areas. I stood there transfixed and robotic. My body felt like a cuttlebone made out of dust, ready to crumble at the slightest indication of his presence. I felt as though I was in another dimension.

"Did you want a snack or something?" my cousin asked. *A snack?* I almost laugh out loud but then shiver instead. *I'm standing inside the home of the man that tried to rape me. Where my last memory of this home is one of me at fourteen years old being woken up in the middle of the night by the sound of the door handle wiggling back and forth by an unknown person on the other side.* I don't want to be in the house any longer and can suddenly feel his hands on my body like an army of ghosts touching my back, breasts, and buttocks. I feel his mouth on me, kissing me and licking me. My stomach drops and I feel a sense of urgency to leave suddenly becoming very afraid that he will be home any minute.

"No, but thank you," I reply. "Let's get going. Hopefully, we won't catch any traffic." I start walking out of the room with my arms crossed in front of my body, scared stiff and putting one foot in front of the other. We were there a few minutes more before we got into the car and headed back to my Aunt Bianca's house.

Each time I travelled to the US to see family, I didn't see Lyle as per the agreement and didn't have to worry that I'd run into him. It was surreal being reassured over and over again at different times by Tamara, that I should not worry about seeing Lyle. *What does she know? What does she think happened? How is Lyle defending himself? Why doesn't she care?* These thoughts would run through my mind trying to make sense of my world yet there was no sense to be made.

My mental health would plummet each time I would encounter anyone from my Aunt Bianca's family either by a visit or phone call. I would feel more worthless and confused and intrusive thoughts would run rampant in my mind. Why didn't my parents care about what he did? *Because you're not important.* Why didn't they care about me enough to take a stand? *Because you're not worth it.* What do my parents really think of me? *They think you're a slut that asked for it.* Month after month, year after year, decade after decade, these thoughts had a permanent fixture in my brain and affected each and every decision I made. Although the sexual abuse stopped long ago, the impact it had followed me every day.

It was over, but the subliminal messages that I had picked up were still part of who I was. Because my self-worth was so damaged and my view of what was acceptable or not was skewed, I found myself consistently gravitating towards men that were abusive or men that had had a plethora of issues. The behaviour accepted from these relationships would reinforce the feelings of worthlessness and shame. What I didn't realize was that invertedly over the years I was taught that abuse was acceptable and normal. As a result, I only felt comfortable in very volatile and dangerous situations. It became the norm for me to become involved with people that were either emotionally, mentally or physically abusive, had substance abuse problems or were involved in criminal activity. I would focus on saving them, changing them or changing myself so that they would choose a life with me. I wanted people that couldn't love themselves to love me instead. These relationships would always end in disaster and in some instances, put me in dangerous situations. Throughout this time, my anxiety and self-destructive behaviors never went away and the only thing that kept me going was that I had an apartment, a vehicle and I lived alone knowing I could have peace inside my four walls.

"Hi, it's me."

"What do you want?"

"My camera. I wanted my camera back. You can keep the photocard, but I wanted to pick up my camera."

"Why is your camera so fucking important to you? You

know what? I don't give a fuck. I'll be home later, come by later."

"Ok." Click. *Well at least I'm getting my camera back and after this, it's done.* I had been dating Jason on and off for years and we had moved in together, but cohabitation didn't last long. I quickly came to wonder if our living arrangement was not for us to move forward in the relationship, but a means for him to indulge more frequently in his addictions. He had lied to me about the money he'd been making, leaving me to pay most of the bills. After I left, the house became a place where he and his friends would congregate and drink themselves into a stupor. As usual I thought Jason might change because of my sudden departure, and as usual I believed my own lies.

A few hours after speaking with Jason I got into my car and drove to our old place. The lights were on in the house and I saw his friends though the front window. *Great.* I thought, realizing he was not home alone. I park and walk up the driveway to knock on the door. As soon as I step on the landing I hear a yell from inside telling me to "Come in!" I open the door and walk into the entryway. When I look up the first set of eyes to meet mine are Jason's. I instantly regret being there. I felt as though I'm on display. I can tell he's inebriated and in a bad mood as he always is after drinking too much and everyone else in the house is intoxicated too. I want to leave immediately but have no excuse to leave so I shut the door behind me instead. His friends chat with me trying to make small talk. I feel tense and respond to their questions keeping my answers short, devoid of opportunity for more discussion. Jason is looking at me the entire time with disdain. I don't know why he is looking at me the way he is, but I pretend not to notice. After a few minutes he tells me my camera is downstairs, so

I head to the basement to get it. Jason doesn't follow me and I'm thankful he stays where he is. *This may be easier than I thought.* My legs are shaking as I walk past everyone in the room, hating to be in an environment where people seemed to lack control.

The basement is a mess. There is garbage everywhere, clothes piled up on chairs and cigarette butts overflowing the ashtrays. I start looking around for any signs of the camera I bought myself for my birthday. *I never should have let him borrow it. I can't believe I let him borrow it. It's probably broken and I'm sure I won't see the money for it.* I hear a noise and look up. I see Jason making his way slowly down the basement stairs, holding on to the wall to steady himself. *Shit,* I think.

"Hey!" I say with a bright smile. "I can't seem to find it but I'm sure you know where it is." Jason walks slowly into the room and doesn't pay much attention to me. He is acting strange and talking to himself trying to find the camera.

"Here it is," he says after a minute of poking it around and handing it to me.

"Thank you," I respond.

Slowly, Jason walks to the other side of the room seemingly still looking for something. "Did you have fun while I was away?" he asks. I stare at him confused. "I'm pretty sure you had more fun on vacation than I did at work," I tell him. He looks at me and chuckles. There is dead silence while he stands on the other side of the room staring at me. "You miss me?" he asks. "Yes, of course I did," I respond. *Great, here we go. He's going to find a reason to get mad at me.* I suddenly feel my body tensing up. Jason bends over near a bar stool and looks like he's trying to pick something up off the floor. His movements are clumsy, and I hope he doesn't fall. The stools used to be upstairs when we lived together, but were brought down to the basement after I left. They were sturdy and made entirely of steel except for the sparkly red vinyl seat. *As soon as he finishes whatever he's doing, I'll leave,* I decide while looking at him. I turn my head towards the back door to check if it's open. I hear a sound and turn to look at Jason from across the room and see him lifting one of the stools above his head. I stare in disbelief as the foot of the stool pierces the ceiling tile. I barely have a chance to react before I see the stool flying across the room in my direction. I duck as it swooshes past my body and into the wall behind me. I stand up and yell, "What the fuck are you doing?!" Jason is looking at me, defiant. His eyes are wide. *He's out of his mind,* I think before running out the back door of the house. Once I reach the driveway and realize Jason did not follow I sit in my car taking a few breaths to calm down. *He could have fucking killed me,* I thought. *He could have fucking killed me.* I am shaking uncontrollably and wait a few minutes for my insides to slow down before starting up my car and leaving. I drive home wondering why I continue to somehow end up in these situations.

A few days later Jason calls while I'm at work. "How are you?" he asks. "Fine," I say. "I would have been worse if you had better aim the other night." "What?" Jason says. *He doesn't even remember,* I think. "The chair you flung at me from across the room," I respond. Dead silence. I pull the phone away from my ear to see if the call is still going. It is. I put the phone back to my ear. "I don't remember that at all," Jason whispers. "I think I'm going to be sick."

I don't respond as I don't know what to say. More silence and then a minute later. "Did I really do that? Is that why you haven't called me?" My silence tells him everything he needs to hear. "I'm so sorry," he says. "I'm so, so sorry," his voice cracks and I can hear him becoming emotional. Hearing him on the phone that way singes me. *He didn't mean to do that. He didn't mean to hurt me. He's upset right now. He loves me. He's just hurting right now and in a bad place. Maybe this will be his wake-up call. Maybe it's this. Maybe this is the moment I've been waiting for. Maybe now he'll treat me differently. Yes. Yes for sure this is it,* I think. "I gotta go," Jason says quietly breaking the silence on the phone. "I'll call you when I'm off work."

"Okay. We'll talk later," I respond and hang up the phone knowing we won't. I don't care though. I know he'll come around sooner or later and am more confident he will after what just transpired. I know I will be worth his love and care someday and if it is not today it will be tomorrow. I get back to work hoping the day will go by quickly. I am comfortable in the life and lies I created. I accepted ill treatment from people that were supposed to care about me with their behavior almost like a motivator for me to 'be better.' The worse I would be treated, the more attached I would become in my relationships.

EIGHT

COCKAMAMIE OF THE NORTH

Years later I am somewhere else, in another town, in another city. I meet someone named Lyle and fall in love with him quickly and easily. The name jarred me at first, but I over-looked it. He was so comfortable to be around, hilariously funny and absolutely charming. He was kind to me and horrified when I told him my story of the abuse and how my family dealt with it. Unlike my last relationship, I felt Lyle wanted to spend time with me and that I didn't have to prove anything to him. I felt constantly pushed away by my ex, but Lyle did not make me feel that way at all. He was always happy to be with me and I felt protected. We vowed to be there for each other and to create a little family of our own where our children would not need to suffer abandon-ment like we did. I told him my secrets and he told me his. He was accused of being violent by his ex-partner and told me about it. We talked and I could not see how could such a kind, gentle man be so misunderstood and seen as an abuser? He was perfect. *What was wrong with him?* I thought.

. . .

"What do you think I should make for dinner tonight with the neighbours? I was thinking I could make some pasta, but I wanted to make something else as well. Do you think they would like short ribs?" I look over at Lyle sitting on the couch playing video games. I'm sure he hears me, he is just not responding. I turn the pages of my cookbook considering other options. A few minutes later I try again.

"I think I may make short ribs. What do you think about that?" I look towards him. He is staring at the TV and intent on whatever he is doing so I continue to think about what to make and decide on short ribs and take notes on my phone. When I'm finished I stand up from the kitchen chair and Lyle makes his way over to me.

"So, what are you going to make?" he asks.

"I decided on short ribs and need to get to the grocery store to get a few more things," I answer.

"Why don't you sit down," Lyle asks, "let's think about this together." I look at him and my stomach does a flip. He looks upset about something, but I have no idea what. "It's okay," I reassure him, "I want to make the short ribs and I'm sure they'll like them." Lyle is staring at me from the seated position he took at the kitchen table after entering the room. His hands are clasped in front of him, and he is staring intently. "Sit down. Why can't you sit down? Just because I didn't jump to your beck and call a minute ago there is no reason you should be acting like this," he says to me.

I stare at him blankly. "Acting like what?" I respond.

"The way you are. You are pissed off because I didn't answer you when I was sitting on the couch. I'm really sick of this shit," he says sharply.

I furrow my brow, "I really don't know what you're talking about," I respond. "I'm not angry at all. I just asked what you thought, but I've made up my mind and need to head over to the store. No big deal." I take a few steps to head to the front door and out of nowhere, Lyle pushes his chair back, quickly pinning my body between the closet door and the chair he is sitting on. I try to move the chair that is pressing hard into my hip and as I do he suddenly bolts up from his own chair, fists clenched, arms down, and starts screaming at me. "YOU WANNA PUSH ME?! I'LL FUCKING KILL YOU BEFORE YOU KILL ME, YOU FUCKING BITCH! FUCK YOU! YOU WANT TO PUSH? I'LL FUCKING KILL YOU! I'LL FUCKING KILL YOU!" I try to get out of his way but within milliseconds, he's pushing my forehead with his forehead so hard that I am forced backwards into the counter. I cannot free myself from his head grip. He is pushing so hard that I feel the corners of the cabinets piercing the back of my head. My hands are gripping the countertop behind me as I try to get leverage to push his forehead off mine, but I am having no luck as I attempt to move sideways or anywhere away from him. He is yelling at me the entire time, spitting while he's screaming, "WHO THE FUCK DO YOU THINK YOU ARE?! I'LL FUCKING KILL YOU!" I am terrified and have no idea what is going on. The force he is using on me is unrelenting and as I slide sideways along the counter, he uses his limbs to box me in. I am hardly breathing and try to scream above him, but my voice is barely above a whisper. "Lyle, you're hurting me, please stop. You're hurting me. Please." I am so scared that I can't speak, and I hear him screaming, "FUCK YOU! FUCK YOU! YOU STUPID CUNT! I'LL FUCKING KILL YOU!" I slide my way over to the fridge all the while holding the counter so that my head is not pushed completely back. Lyle is pushing so hard that the fridge gives way and removes me from his headlock. I turn towards the kitchen window and see that it's open.

As soon as I try to scream I see Lyle's hand clamp over my face covering my mouth and nose and feel his other hand holding the back of my neck. He is leaning my head back and my eyes are towards ceiling. I am struggling and squirming trying to get out of his grip. His voice changes to a violent whisper, "SHUT THE FUCK UP! SHUT UP! SHUT UP! SHUT UP." I could not say a word if I tried. His hand is smothering my face and I begin to panic. As I struggle to breath he looks into my eyes and moves his pinkie finger away from my nostrils, leaving the majority of his hand still on my mouth. "QUIET!" he insists. Instead, I open my mouth and bite down HARD on his fingers covering my upper lip. He jumps away, releasing me from his grasp and holding his bitten finger. "Fuck! Fuck! Fuck!" I hear him say. I run out of the house and end up at the park down the street. I am breathing hard and see a nearby bench where I go to steady myself. *What the fuck just happened?* I think wildly. *He has never laid a finger on me before, and he just tried to choke me?* I was in disbelief.

I sit on the bench to calm my nerves. I have no idea what to do. We have been living together for over a year and a half and he had never been aggressive towards me. Sure, he slammed doors, cabinets, punched walls, threw my things and broke things when he was upset, but that was no big deal right? He never did anything to me physically, so it was fine. Abuse is only when someone does something to you physically, like punch you. Not someone that tries to stop you from screaming. After talking to myself and rationalizing what happened I decide to go back home not recognizing that what he was doing and how I was responding was not rational. As I walk through the door and into the kitchen I see Lyle sitting at the table with his head down. "I'm sorry. I'm so sorry. Please forgive me, I'm so sorry." Lyle reaches for my hand, and I let him take it. He promises that he'll never do anything like that again. "Never again," he says to me holding my hands and looking into my eyes. "Please don't leave me." I feel sad and angry that I have this type of memory with us. I felt before this point that my relationship with Lyle was the one that would be different, but now there is this awful memory and event that I don't know what to do with. I feel terrible that he is so upset and tell him it's okay. I know it's not okay, but I tell him it's okay for me, and for him. I believe it is a one-time thing and I believe he will never harm me again. I don't understand abuse even if I think I do. It is open season again, but this time with someone different. I cancel the dinner plans for that evening and reschedule.

I arrive home from work later that week and the living room is decorated with a beautiful picture I said I liked and that we had been eyeing together. He smiles as I enter the room. "Do you like it?" he asks, motioning to the canvas on the wall. "That looks incredible," I respond with a smile. He smiles back at me, and we carry on as if nothing happened.

A year or so later we decide to go on vacation to reconnect. I was becoming increasingly afraid of him and his outbursts so on a few occasions, when I feared his wrath or could not predict his irritability level, I left and went to stay with my parents. I did not want to leave him, but I also didn't know what to do. We had briefly touched upon him seeing a therapist but that resulted in him purchasing an anger management workbook. He said if I could heal my agoraphobia with a workbook then he could figure out to how to control his anger. I felt insulted that he grouped such a monumental achievement of mine with his half-assed attempt at addressing his own issues that he did not want to admit to. It was clear he had absolutely no concept of how hard I worked to extract myself from my cycles by changing my habits. Eventually during another argument, he tore up the workbook yelling that he didn't need this shit and blamed me for his violent outbursts, accusing me of instigating arguments with whatever he felt I was doing wrong at the time. I of course, would listen to him and figure that if I behaved better somehow, then we wouldn't have these problems.

We woke early that day to go sightseeing, but between the jet lag and chronic anxiety I had that had once again developed, I was not feeling the greatest. My head was a bit foggy, but I shook it off and figured I'd feel more alive once we were on the road and I was caffeinated. I wanted to move on with each day as quickly as possible looking forward to the vacation being over. I never wanted to go in the first place as I was feeling increasingly trapped and oppressed by his behavior. I was genuinely afraid of him and made arrangements with a friend prior to leaving that I would contact him if I needed to return back to the country immediately alone, without Lyle.

"We'll need to get some gas at least once so why don't we do that first?" asks Lyle.

"Okay, sounds good," I respond.

We pull up to the gas station and Lyle parks the car in front of the pump. As he gets out of the car he leaves his prescription sunglasses on the seat. I stare at them thinking to pick them up but decide against it in case my touching his glasses sets him off somehow.

"Hey, I need your pin code out here!" I hear Lyle say loudly outside of the car. I get out and approach him while he's speaking. He tells me that it's a pre-pay pump but all he needs is my credit card pin. I stand next to him in front of the pump and stare at the screen. My mind goes blank. I cannot for the life of me remember the code. Why can I not remember? "I can't remember," I whisper to myself.

"What did you say? What do you mean you can't remember?" Lyle asks. I continue to stare at the keypad concentrating. My hands don't even remember the movement associated with my pin. My mind is completely blank, and I feel myself getting shaky. I make an attempt and access is denied. Lyle looks at me uneasily. I take a breath and feel dread as I know I will make another failed attempt. I try again and access is denied. "Don't do it again, we'll go to another gas station and hopefully by then you'll remember," he says.

The look on his face tells me he's angry "Okay, I'm sorry. I just can't remember in this moment." I look to the ground and make my way back into the car. I try to control the panic I feel for having forgotten. *What if I don't remember by the time we get to the next gas station?* I take a breath as I feel an anxiety attack coming on making me feel woozy. I take a few more breaths and concentrate on regulating myself while Lyle goes into the gas station store for water.

When he returns, he opens the car door and sits on his seat, crushing his glasses. I gasp as he rolls his eyes shifting in his seat to get the glasses out from under him. When they are in his hands, he begins to scream in the car, at the top of his lungs, while bending and breaking the glasses even more. "FUCK! FUCK! FUCK!" He is screaming, and his hands are working hard to break the glasses apart. He gives up, and to my horror, turns the ignition on and starts driving. While constantly screaming and driving he punches the windshield and I see his hand bend the tempered glass outwards. The windshield shatters completely in seconds and I brace myself as he continues to drive and scream. I yell at him to stop the car. He is yelling over me but I cannot understand a word he is saying while he is driving erratically all over the road. *I am going to die,* I think. *This is how I am going to die.* I look at my door and unlock it, thinking I can jump out of the car somehow, but Lyle is swerving the car closer and closer to the stone walls lining the road and into oncoming traffic. "STOP DRIVING! STOP DRIVING! PLEASE STOP DRIVING! PULL OVER!" I am begging him to stop the car. He drives and continues to yell until he swerves into an empty parking lot. He stops yelling as suddenly as he started, exits the car and makes his way towards a nearby tree line. I breathe a sob of relief as I see him walking away and open the car door for air. I heave a few times but do not vomit. I look around and he is nowhere to be seen. Twenty minutes later I see Lyle walking back to the car. He is walking slowly, his shoulders sagged, and his head is down. I don't know what to do. I am scared to approach him, and I am scared to stay seated in the car. He stops walking and sits down on a curb his head pointing to the ground.

I wait a few seconds and slowly make my way over to sit down next to him. This time he does not apologize or promise me that he will stop the behavior. I put my arm around his shoulders and assure him that we will take care of the car, and this is just a bump in the road. He lifts his head, looks into my eyes and says, "What I care about is that this will be what you remember when you leave me." I am stunned by his words and do not have anything to say. In that moment I hug him with a tug of war inside of me wanting to walk away in that instant, but also feeling empathy for the tremendous mistake he knew he just made. I assure him that I won't go anywhere and in that moment I do not lie.

We discuss how we are going to fix the car and how we are going to move on with the vacation despite this bump in the road.

"I'm leaving him," I say to Annie. "I'm done." She stares back at me and shakes her head. "Are you sure? This time for good?" Annie asks. I look at her and nod. We are in the garage whispering as I am afraid Lyle may have placed recording devices in the home we share. He had done so before, and I didn't see why he wouldn't do it again. I explain to her that I had come to understand Lyle was telling friends and family that I was suffering from a mental illness and our relationship was bearing the brunt of it. Furthermore, Lyle's mother was an active participant in the smear campaign, informing people that he couldn't leave me since he felt so guilty to do so in my time of need. "I can't accept it," I said. "I can't accept that to hide his own issues he is lying to people about me. And furthermore, his mother is in on it too." I shake my head in disbelief. "I am done with all of this. It's obvious he has turned completely against me so what am I doing here?" Once again I thought I was in a family with someone, but that family I tried to create completely betrayed me.

It took a few weeks to get organized after I resolved to leave for good. I found a place to live with the intention of waiting until Lyle's business trip to move. I was not going to tell him I was leaving as I was afraid of his reaction and could never predict whether he was on the precipice of slamming a cabinet in frustration or going into his gun locker stored in the closet. I checked the area where Lyle stored bullets and saw that they hadn't been touched in a long time. I didn't disturb their position and kept my eye on any changes while throwing out the trash a few times a week. I found an apartment, was able to keep my job and be far enough away from him so we wouldn't run into each other.

Everything was planned and organized for me to leave, but I felt increasingly guilty as my departure date got closer. I didn't want to leave in the way I was intending to, but it was the safest scenario I could come up with. I wrote a letter and contacted a close friend of his asking for suggestions, but was told that they had known he was abusive for a long time and that they too thought leaving the letter was safest way for me to leave.

My parents suggested I move in with them, but I wasn't interested. Their distorted reality would not help me at all, and I was never relaxed or felt safe around them. Their treatment of me and the way they handled the abuse was a thorn I could never pull out of my side no matter how much time had passed. Also, my dad's behavior towards my mother was something I knew I could not tolerate if I were to put myself in that environment again, especially now.

———

He wanted onion buns but they're not fresh, I thought staring at the lack of selection in the store. *The ones without the onions are fresher. Maybe I'll just get plain instead of the onion ones. No, forget it. I'll get both so he has nothing to get upset about.* I catch myself worried about the choice of bread and am embarrassed. *How the hell did I get here, where I'm in a grocery store fearing his wrath if I get the wrong bread?* I am embarrassed and scold myself, *you are worthless and stupid. It's no wonder you ended up in this mess.* As I make my way up to the register I greet the cashier and smile and say, "Nothing like sandwiches for dinner!" She looks at me and smiles. "Why not?" she says returning my smile. I feel jittery and quickly busy myself with collecting my groceries. I pay for my items and drive home to see that his truck is not yet parked on the driveway. I enter the house, change out of my work clothes, and make my way to the kitchen to prep for dinner. As I am entering the kitchen, I hear Lyle unlocking the front door.

"Hello! I bought two types of buns for us for dinner. How was your day?" I say.

"It was okay. I'm so hungry." Lyle says. He places his things down and joins me at the kitchen counter to put the sandwiches together. "You could have maybe gotten staler bread don't you think?" Lyle asks.

My tone is playful, "Well maybe you should have gotten it yourself!" I say while turning to him.

Suddenly Lyle raises his fist and slams it down on the counter so hard everything flies up into the air and lands on the floor. "FUCK!" He screams at the top of his lungs. I run away from him to the other side of the kitchen. My legs are shaking, and I am waiting for what he's going to do next. He is looking towards the ceiling and his back is facing me. He doesn't look at me and walks away and up the stairs. I stand there paralyzed. *Is he getting a gun?* I wait to hear what he is doing. *If he goes into the bedroom where the gun locker is, I'll run.* I sit down at the head of the kitchen table and wait. I sigh in relief when I hear him descending the stairs after having not gone into the bedroom that housed the gun locker. "LOOK what you did!' Lyle says pointing to his hand. I look to see the hand he used to punch the counter, wrapped up in a towel. I have no idea what is wrong with it.

"I'm sorry," I say softly. "YOU'RE SORRY? YOU SHOULD BE SORRY! THIS IS WHAT YOU DID TO ME. DO YOU SEE THAT AT ALL? *YOU DID THIS! YOU DID THIS TO ME!*" Lyle yells pointing at his hand. I stay seated, watching him and repeating the words "I'm sorry, I'm so sorry. I didn't mean to do that. I'm sorry," all the while thinking, *I just need to get out of here. I am so close to getting out of here, I just need to survive this moment.* Lyle stops yelling at me and goes into the living room. The house is quiet. After a few minutes I take a deep breath and slowly exhale. I get up from the chair and clean up the items that have fallen to the floor before going over and sitting down next to him to apologize and comfort him all the while repeating in my head, *It's almost over. It's almost over. It's almost over. Soon I will be free from his presence and in peace.*

The next day after work Lyle arrives home asking me to drive us to the hospital. His hand swelled to twice its size and he wanted to have x-rays done. On our way to the hospital, Lyle makes sure our stories coincide. "I'll tell them I was splitting a steak in two and my hand slammed into the cutting board too hard." Lyle suggests. "Sure," I say with no emotion. "I will follow your lead." Lyle nods his head at me in satisfaction.

Once at the hospital, Lyle tells his steak story, and the doctors find it strange that so much damage was caused by separating steaks. "Yep! Just making dinner and this is what happens!" Lyle jokes with the doctors. One of them looks over at me and I stare back into his eyes hoping to ward off any doubts he may have regarding Lyle's story. *Please don't question me, please don't question me, please don't question me.* I repeat in my head until the doctor looks away.

"Well," the doctor says to Lyle, "it looks like you broke your hand in a few places, and we'll need to reset it. Once that's over you'll need the hand in a cast for at least six weeks."

"To reset do you mean break my hand again?" Lyle asks.

"Yes. That is what we will have to do." The doctor responds. *Wow* I think, grateful that I was going to see karma in action. *Good thing I wasn't in the way of that one. At least now I won't have to worry about him hurting me before I leave.* After Lyle's hand is reset I step away to the bathroom and on my way back one of the doctors that was working with Lyle stops me. "Is everything ok? I think you passed his room. It's over there," he says pointing behind him. "Funny how much damage can result in making dinner," the doctor says while staring into my eyes once again. I smile and respond, "Yes. It's really funny isn't it? Is the cast on yet?" I ask changing the subject quickly. The doctor keeps staring at me and I stare back. We lock eyes and there is a pause. "Yes. He's ready to go home," the doctor finally says.

"Great! I say enthusiastically. Thank you for all of your care." I smile as I walk away from him. There was no way I was putting myself into any more danger. I was all set up to leave and that was my plan. To safely slip out of this horrendous life I was in and never look back.

A few weeks later, while Lyle is on a business trip I coordinate a moving company to come in to assist with a quick pack-up and move. Before locking up the house for good, I leave Lyle a letter on the kitchen counter and complete a scan of the house, but there is nothing left that I value. I spot one of the many gifts Lyle gave me after one of his abusive episodes and smile knowing I'll never have to see that reminder or him ever again.

Lyle arrives home a few days later enraged that I have left and ordering me on the phone to come back home. *I am home,* I think placing the phone down on my bed, so I don't have to hear his yelling in my ear. My cat Lucy jumps up onto the bed beside me letting me know she's there. She begins purring and I pet her belly feeling the vibrations she is making. I listen to his screaming through the phone like a television that is in another room, muffled and unclear. I listen for any pauses in case I need to respond and keep petting Lucy around her neck and ears making sure she receives the love she deserves. I listen to the sound of his voice drone on and then hear him hang up. A minute later he calls me back and yells at me some more and continues to do so over and over again. I sit on my bed, but he is going on and on, hanging up and calling me back demanding I come home. At one point I hear his mother's voice screaming in the background asking me why I left her son. She sounds inebriated again and I am even more convinced of my decision. There was no way I was going to survive in that situation.

I stare at the numbers on the paper in my hand. It had been months since I left Lyle, and I was slowly recovering. The rejection and abandonment I felt, despite me being the one leaving was tearing me up. It was clear Lyle left the relationship far earlier than when I physically left, and I didn't understand it. Why did he abandon me? Why did he turn against me? Am I really the one that instigated his treatment of me? Was I really the problem? *This couldn't all be me.* I thought while blindly dialing the numbers. *I know I have issues, but I didn't imagine the abuse.*

"Hello. Alicia speaking." I heard a feminine voice on the other end of the line.

Holy shit it's her. "Um, hi," I say nervously. "Alicia?"

"Yes. Alicia here."

Here goes nothing. I can't believe she picked up. "Hey, Alicia, I'm Rosemary. Lyle's partner. Well, EX-partner," I add quickly. "I left, and we haven't had contact in months. I know this is completely out of the blue, but would you mind if I asked you some questions? I won't take up much of your time and he's completely out of the picture, so you needn't worry about him lurking around. He spoke so much about you that I knew where you worked, and I wanted to reach you. I understand it's weird, but I mean no harm." The phone is silent. *She hasn't hung up.*

"What is it that you want to know? Do you know how weird this is?" Alicia asks. "Are you sure this is not a joke?"

"No. It's definitely not a joke. I left a few months ago and haven't had contact with him. I asked that he send all communication in writing and so far he has not contacted me. I'm sure he won't either." I tell her. "He thinks I'm cra-"

"Oh, wait let me guess. He thinks you are crazy. He's labelling you as crazy?" Alicia asks. "Join the club."

"Yes," I respond. "He absolutely is labeling me as crazy," I say hypnotically. *She was the crazy one too.* I thought recalling all the times he told me, his friends and anyone that would listen that she was certifiably insane.

"Anyone that leaves him or does something wrong is his eyes is labelled as crazy. It's never him or his actions that are wrong. It's always someone else's fault," Alicia says.

I take a deep breath and exhale. I can't believe I had her on the phone. "I'm sorry if this is abrupt or if this brings back any memories but I'd really like to know. Was Lyle abusive to you in any way when you were together?"

"Ohh ya!" Alicia responds. "That man has something severely wrong with him. I was not the best person to him, and I made some big mistakes, but I'm so glad it's over. He scared me. He still scares me."

We spoke for well over an hour and exchanged experiences discussing our respective relationships. There were so many similarities between our two stories and so many moments of validation giving me the confidence I needed to accept that although I was not perfect, he had absolutely no idea how to regulate his emotions or outbursts or deal with his own demons. There was no way the relationship could have worked. Ever.

I felt myself starting to breathe easier and at the end of the conversation thanked her for helping me and she in turn thanked me for helping her. The conversation changed my perspective on many things and provided validation of my suspicion that Lyle had exaggerated his ex's behavior to cover up his own issues. I never understood why he had always put so much energy into convincing people of his ex's mental disorder, but now it all made much more sense. There were so many red flags to warn me about him, but I kept ignoring them and stuffing them somewhere else so as not to see them. Thankfully, it was over.

NINE

TURN AND BURN

"We were all surprised that you became so serious with Lyle. For someone like you and with all the problems you had, we never thought you'd get serious with anyone. Clearly, he wasn't the one, but I'm sure he exists." I couldn't believe what I was hearing. *Problems I have? How dare you?* I thought. I bit my lip to hold my tongue. *I don't have the stomach for this shit* I thought. I don't know why I picked up the phone when my cousin Tamara called. I was having a perfectly wonderful Saturday afternoon at home on my couch, reading a book and listening to music. Each time I would speak with her or have contact with anyone from Aunt Bianca's family, the cycle of self-hate, loathing and shame would rev itself back up again and begin its voyage in the labyrinth of my body and mind for the next week or two, depending on my self-esteem.

I wanted to scream at her and tell her my 'problems' involved processing and coping with what her husband did to me while my family brushed it all aside and pretended it didn't happen. My 'problems' involved coping with the impact of his actions within a family environment that dismissed my call for help, ridiculed me for my reaction to the abuse, and then shunned me as though I was defective. I wanted to explain to her that my problems had nothing to do with me and that my problems were a result of other people's problems being projected onto me. I wanted to clarify that my lack of reaction when her husband abused me was not an invitation but a response to the trauma I was enduring. I wanted her to know that such an accusation was really a confession and that more often than not when you are accused of something, you can be sure that it is some-thing your accuser has done, would do or is thinking of doing. I want to explain to her that there was nothing wrong with me. There was never anything wrong with me. I wanted to say all of this, but instead I bite my lip and let her talk about whatever she wanted to. I look over at the clock to decide what time it will be in exactly five minutes because that's when I'll tell her I need to get going. I'm not inter-ested in anything she has to say.

"Hey, Rose, can you pick me up and take me to the hospital?" I hear my brother Joseph say as I answer his call.

"Why? What's wrong?' I ask frantically.

"Nothing don't worry. I need to get there as the clinic needs to change the dressings on my foot injury. Lia will be picking me up on her way home from work. I just need a ride there," he answers.

"Yeah, sure of course!" I respond. I turn to look at Chris and he nods. I end the call and we begin walking towards the exit of the store we were in. I had recently moved into a new apartment and was shopping for some lighting when my brother called. Chris and I had been dating a few months and I thought things were moving in the right direction. I felt like my new apartment was a fresh start and I was happy to be back in my neighborhood and grateful for meeting someone like Chris. He was kind, patient, sincere, and treated me with empathy, warmth, and respect. He was also fun and easy to be with and was gently coaxing me out of my shell.

Chris and I get into the car and drive my brother to the hospital. As I drop him off, I tell him I'm close by, and to call if he needs anything. He doesn't call but my mother does a few hours later to tell me that my brother is staying at the hospital overnight.

"How come? He was fine when I dropped him off. All he needed was his bandages to be changed," I tell her.

"I don't know, Rose," my mother responds with a sigh, "He just said that the doctors saw something, and they wanted to keep him overnight for observation."

"Oh. Okay," I reply. I end the call a few minutes later and try not to panic. Chris looks at me and reassures me not to worry unless there is something to worry about, and that my brother is in the best place if something is wrong. *He's right,* I think. I walk into the kitchen but the phone rings again and it's Lia. "Hey, Rose, can you go to my house and keep an eye on the girls 'til I get home?" she asks.

"Sure. I reply, "I can leave in ten minutes." I look over at Chris, but he is up already and waiting for us to leave. "Where are we going?" he asks.

Within a few days of Joseph's hospital visit, we are told there are a few blockages in his arteries and that surgery will most likely be what is needed to fix the problem. A week later surgeons try to insert stents in his arteries but are not successful, ultimately scheduling my brother for triple bypass, open heart surgery on December 23rd. During a time when the world chattered about a virus that was spreading and was causing casualties oceans away, Joseph successfully survived the impact of the surgery and trauma to his body. In those weeks that my brother was in the hospital, seeing him on the verge of death shocked me into the realization of how incredibly fragile each one of us are. I watched him struggle for his life from one day to the next and I understood how easily someone can just blink, and never open their eyes again.

I don't want to live with these secrets anymore, I wake in the middle of the night with the thought pounding through my brain like spotlights on a dark highway. I am lying on my back and Lucy is at the foot of my bed. I look over at her, and the silhouette of her feline head stares back at me curious as to why I am awake. "I'm okay," I tell her, while caressing her head before settling back to sleep. I comfort myself with the thought that Joseph was leaving the hospital soon and that things would be returning back to normal.

A few days after Joseph arrives home from the hospital I call Chris to check in on him since he was home with the flu. Chris doesn't respond but sends me a text message a little while later that reads *'Didn't have a good sleep. Tossed and turned, trying to fall asleep.'* I text back letting him know it sucks that he's sick, and that I definitely knew what tossing and turning felt like. I make a mental note to call him later that day but when I do he doesn't respond. *He's probably just catching up on sleep,* I think to myself.

Later at home I check the time and it's 9:00 p.m. Chris hasn't sent a text message or called, and I can't shake the feeling that something was wrong. I turn the TV off in my apartment and pick up my cell phone to see if it's working. Obviously, it is, just like it was an hour before when I checked it. *This is not like him,* I think. *This is really not like him.* I want to reach out to his family and figure that if I'm to send a text or call, this would be the time to do it. I send a quick message to his sister but don't receive a response until hours later when it is clear something has gone terribly wrong.

"He's had a stroke. We need to operate to release the pressure in his skull. We need to do this to save his life. He may never speak or walk again. We need to work fast though, the swelling in his brain is not a good sign." I am spinning listening to the doctors. *What is happening? Why is this happening? He's a good person, he's young, he's full of life. He just had the flu. He was getting better. How did he have a stroke? What is a stroke?* I don't understand any of it but all that keeps barreling through my mind once again is the fragility of our existence and how we can be extinguished immediately, without warning and without question.

Chris ultimately survived the stroke, but his body and brain suffered damage which made it impossible for him to fully recover. I watched him struggle to speak and walk while doctors told me that he could understand everything that was being said, however the language disorder he had developed called aphasia, was the obstacle that was blocking him. I could not imagine being silenced in such a way as to be incapable of expressing oneself. It terrified me and drove me deeper into self-reflection.

I don't want to live with these secrets anymore, I think again as I end a call with my mother. *I don't want to die without telling anyone what happened to me.* It is a few days after Mother's Day and my mom had called upset that Uncle Elio had been in the hospital. "What happened?" I ask.

"It had to do with Lyle. Uncle Elio said something to Lyle and there was an argument. Somehow he fell and almost broke his arm," my mother replied.

"What did Uncle Elio say?"

"Something in reference to what he did to you."

"What are you talking about?" I ask. "Uncle Elio has no idea what really happened to me."

"Yes, but he just said something about how Lyle was not nice to his family in the past. You should see his arm. It's purple. I can't believe it," my mother says sadly. A minute later my mother sends me the photo of my uncle's arm and I see she's right, his entire forearm looks like the colour of an eggplant as though someone took a brush and painted his skin. As I stare at the picture I think of my uncle and see his face in my mind smiling at me with his incredible hazel freckled eyes.

When I was a little girl and used to visit, I would ask him to trade me the Canadian funds I had saved up with his American bills. If I handed him a $20 he would give me back $200 and I would look at him with wide eyes shaking my head no that I couldn't accept it. He would smile and tell me to run along and not worry about it. Each time my father would mention that he needed to exchange money, my brothers and I would pipe up and tell him to ask Uncle Elio. I smiled remembering those moments and then felt a surge of anger looking at the photo of his arm.

I end the call enraged with Lyle and completely beside myself asking once again how on earth this monster keeps hurting my family in one way or another. My mother had mentioned in the conversation that Tamara tried to defend her husband which was what resulted in the argument. I had no idea what really happened since I wasn't there, but I had reached a limit. I was done with the toxicity of my Aunt Bianca's family and done with keeping Lyle's secrets so I sat down to write a letter to Tamara and twenty minutes later, I sat back in the chair and stared at the screen. I thought it would have taken longer to write, but the words came to me much more quickly than expected.

Dear Tamara,

I heard what went on the other day and although I wasn't there I understand that your dad was hurt because you were in the midst of defending your husband. I thought I'd write to you, my cousin, blood of my blood, so that you can have an understanding of what you are defending. I don't expect a response or acknowledgement. I have never had any response that has satisfied any of the hurts so I will not expect one now. Any responses I did receive from family simply strengthened my feelings of confusion and abandonment, as well as taught me that despite the black and white of situations, grey is really what exists when it comes to keeping the peace in the family, and that peace will be kept at any cost.

The only way to say it is this... your husband molested me for 4 years starting when I was 12 years old. The first time it happened you were at my house and sleeping upstairs while I was sleeping in the small

TV room. Your husband came in and watched some TV with me. When the show was over I got up to go to bed and he asked me for a hug. I didn't think anything of it at the time, but when he hugged me he pulled me close and began to run his hands on the sides of my body while touching my breasts. I tried to pull away but he whispered in my ear not to worry and that no one would know. I finally was able to push him off me and I fled upstairs. The next morning, I went skiing with Philip and you left for the airport by the time I came back.

There were many other instances over the years... One night at your place I was sleeping in your den with the door locked and I heard the door handle jingle in the night as if someone was trying to get in. I was terrified as to who was on the other side and didn't open the door as I was sure I knew who it was. Nothing happened that night thankfully but I did lock myself in that room that night on purpose.

The family vacations in Italy became nightmares for me. At the beach house he would enter my bedroom at night and watch me while I slept. One time he sat on my bed and when I woke up terrified, he only left when he thought someone was coming. I recall one specific time where I woke up and he was standing over me leaning into me almost as if he was going to kiss me. I pushed him off me and told him to get away.

He laughed at me and said that he just wanted to kiss me good-bye.

Daily visits to the beach would include his continuous comments about my body when people weren't around to hear him. He asked if he could take naked photos of me over and over again so that he can save them and he complimented me numerous times on my shaving techniques and how my bikini line was so soft and had no stubble. He would ask me repeatedly if he could touch it and I would exit the situation in any way I could, completely paralysed and terrified of him.

The worst of the times was when I was 16 and in Italy. Everyone was there that summer and I thought that it would be ok since there were so many people in the house all the time. I thought he could never get to me but he did. I stayed home from the beach one day because I had my period and I thought he had left to meet up with everyone at the beach before lunch. I went into your mother's apt to make a peanut butter sandwich and my back was turned towards the counter near the fridge so I didn't see him come into the kitchen. Suddenly I felt his body against mine, his hands running all over my body and him kissing my neck and nuzzling my ear. I was paralysed with fear as I was so many times before but I snapped out of it and managed to push him off. I ran upstairs to my mom's bathroom and I locked the door terrified that he would follow me and break the door down or something. I didn't know what to expect from him when he was around.

That same summer I turned 17 and about a week after our arrival home, I told my parents what had been going on for years. The very next day they took me to a shrink as they didn't know what to do with the information or how to handle it. A week or so later we went to the US to confront your husband and it was then that I found out he did things to other women in the family as well. I don't know what my dad said to him that day but I do remember your husband making me feel as if he didn't know what I was talking about when he knew full well the behavior I was referring to. Anyway, at some point after I told my parents, and after my dad confronted your husband, we returned to the US for a party a few months later. I didn't want to go but according to my parents I couldn't stay home and had to attend this party. Your husband was at that party and did not walk by me without calling me a slut, a whore, a liar, a fucking bitch, and whatever other atrocities he was willing to throw at me. Again, I never said anything as I was told not to discuss it. Upon my return back home, I began skipping school and fighting with my parents daily. I didn't know what I wanted them to do to help but it didn't matter because they weren't going to do anything anyway. The way they handled it was to send me to Italy and to ensure I didn't talk to you about it.

Moving forward I left it alone. With my move to Italy I wanted a fresh start and I began to create my life in any way I knew how and with much criticism from others. Over the years I was continuously regarded as some sort of black sheep and my parents continued to pretend all was well. In the meantime, my anxiety disorder worsened to the point of agoraphobia (which thankfully I was able to overcome) yet as you know my anxiety disorder has never gone away.

As an end to this letter I just want to let you know that I'm here to talk if you want but I will not tolerate any anger towards me in any way, shape or form. I am the victim here and I will not permit any maltreatment. If this letter seems devoid of feeling I apologize. This may be new information to you but to me it is not. **If this is not** new information to you, consider this our last communication. If you stood by this and did nothing you and he are the same person to me.

As I stated in the beginning of the email I wanted you to know what you were defending before you defended it. Your husband doesn't deserve to be defended and doesn't deserve one ounce of understanding. He knows what he did and he gets away with

it every single day. In closing I want to
say I'm sorry but I do not have anything to
be sorry about.

I write this letter with a heavy heart
and the only thing I'm sorry for is how
difficult this is for you.

Your cousin,
Rosemary

I read the letter a few times over and save the draft keeping
the details of what he did vague. If she wanted to know
more, she could call me. There was enough information for
what needed to be understood and I realize I am still caught
in a web of shame, feeling as though it was my fault. I stare
at the letter on my screen for a few minutes thinking about
the trajectory of my life from the night he touched me, to
sitting in front of my computer, thirty-five years later, finally
breaking the silence that I've held onto for so long. I feel
scared, and somewhere, I feel relief.

I decide to read it to my brother Joseph before sending it
and select his name on my phone to make the call.

"Hello?"

"Hey, it's me. I wrote the letter to Tamara, and I wanted
to read it to you so you can tell me what you think."

"Sure, go ahead," he responds, "I'm listening." I read the
letter with no interruptions. My brother is quiet on the
phone listening. I am ashamed reading it to him, but I
imagine there are only a few things he doesn't know. After I
finish, the phone line is still silent. "Hello?" I ask, worried
that the line may have cut out.

"Yeah. Um. Send it," Joseph says disjointedly.

"Is it okay?" I ask.

"Yes. I mean. It's good. Send it. I need to go. I'll call you back," Joseph says.

"Well, I may not send it in this instant, but I will send it."

"Yes. Send it. I need to go." Click.

I stare at the phone in my hand. *That was pretty abrupt,* I think. I stand up from the chair and stretch. Dinner needs to be picked up and I was late.

My cell phone rings as I stand in front of the restaurant waiting for my order. The caller ID reads 'Joseph' but when I pick up the phone it's my brother's wife, Lia.

"Hi, Rose. Can you tell me what happened? Your brother isn't able to tell me," Lia asks.

"What do you mean?" I ask her. "Why? Is everything okay? What's wrong?"

"I mean, Joseph hasn't been able to stop crying enough to tell me what happened since you hung up the phone twenty minutes ago. What is going on?" I hear my brother in the background trying to use his voice through his tears, "I didn't know. I didn't know."

"I don't know, Lia," I respond. "I read him the letter that I wrote to Tamara, and he told me to send it." All the while that I'm talking I hear Joseph in the background repeating the words, "I didn't know."

"What letter?" Lia asks.

Suddenly I hear my brother's broken voice much clearer, "I didn't know, I didn't know."

"What didn't you know?" I ask Joseph. My brother does not answer me. He keeps repeating the same phrase. I hear a muffle and Lia again on the phone.

"Rose?" Lia asks.

"Listen, Lia. I'm downtown right now in front of a restaurant waiting for the food I ordered. I don't understand what he's talking about, so I'll just call you when I get back home," I say to her.

"Okay, Rose. Talk soon," she responds ending the call.

What is he talking about? What doesn't he know? Maybe he didn't know about the incident in the kitchen. Maybe my mother didn't tell him that story.

I walk back home with my dinner wondering what Joseph knew. I know that when I told my mother about the abuse I didn't tell her everything. *But I did tell her enough. I told her about the first time it happened when I was twelve and then I told her about the incident in the kitchen and a few other things.*

When I arrive home I reread the letter a few more times to understand what Joseph meant by him 'not knowing' and figure perhaps he didn't know about the incident in Italy when Lyle tried to rape me in the kitchen. I sit in front of my computer and take a deep breath, exhaling as my computer comes back to life. I open the email draft and I stare at the screen with my index finger resting lightly on the mouse while the little hand icon hovers over the word SEND. *If I were to die tomorrow, at least I will not die with this in my heart,* I think. I press send before another thought enters my mind and quickly get up from my chair to head into the kitchen to eat dinner. I had waited long enough to send the letter.

I call Joseph afterwards and he picks up after the first ring. He begins talking immediately.

"I didn't know those things happened to you. Mom told me that all he did was touch you while he was walking by you. She didn't tell me anything that you wrote in the letter."

"What?" I say.

"All I knew and all everyone knew was that he walked

by you at a party or something and he touched you. I had no idea any of this happened," Joseph explained. "Does Mom know everything?"

"Mostly, but yes, she does," I responded in shock. "She knew about most of the incidents in the letter. She knew about the first time, and she knew about some of the other incidents."

We talk for a while on the phone, but nothing is really registering. The only thing that keeps running through my mind is that he didn't know.

"Does Dad know?" Joseph asks, "If I didn't know then Dad wouldn't know either and neither would Philip."

"What are you talking about?" I ask Joseph. "Of course, they know." As soon as the words are out of my mouth I doubt them.

"You need to send the letter to Philip and Dad. Did you read the letter to Mom?" Joseph asks.

"No, I didn't read the letter to Mom and I'm not sending the letter to Philip or Dad. How am I going to send it to Dad? He doesn't have email. I'm not sending it to Philip either. Maybe tomorrow. It's late. I know that they know. I don't know why you don't know but I'm sure they know."

"I really don't think they know. Can you send it to Philip, and I'll call him?" Joseph asks.

"Sure," I respond. All I want to do is get off the phone and be alone. I feel like I'm in a nightmare. *How is this possible? Did my mother really keep everything I told her a secret?*

The next morning I answer the phone to Philip's call. He is also in shock and upset asking questions about things that happened over thirty years ago.

"What did you know?" I asked my brother.

"All I recall is that Mom told me he touched you while you were walking by him. I had no idea that there were different instances over a period of four years. I never understood why it affected you so much, but now I understand. Joseph and I probably had the conversation over a million times. If what he did to you was something that was positioned almost as a misunderstanding, why were you so affected by it? We never understood. No one ever understood."

I listen quietly to him. I feel as though I'm in another dimension. I feel lightheaded and nauseous. *How is this possible? How is it that my brothers didn't know? I told her that he was molesting me for four years. I don't understand. Why didn't my mother tell them what I told her? Why do my brothers think all he did was touch me in passing?* I thought I had felt alone and abandoned before, but now the feelings hit me on an entirely different level realizing how incredibly alone I really was.

"Are you going to read the letter to Dad? You need to tell him," Philip says.

"'I'm sure Dad knows and maybe he just didn't tell you or Joseph," I respond.

"Rosemary, I'm telling you that he doesn't know. I really think you need to speak with him about this," Philip insists.

I take a deep breath in and exhale. "I don't know what I'm going to do. It seems really unbelievable to me that she didn't tell you or Joseph." I am still there. My brain is still there within the shockwave of understanding that my mother kept what I told her under wraps all these years. I was devastated.

A few days later Tamara calls and I stare at the phone until the voicemail icon pops up. When I listen to the message, I hear Tamara's cheerful voice as if all is right in the world, "Hi, Ro, it's Tamara. I'm calling to tell you that my email wasn't working so I just got your email today instead of yesterday. Anyway, when you get this message give me a call. I think you have your facts wrong." *What? What is she talking about? How can the facts be wrong? I know exactly what happened to me.* I listen to the voicemail a few times before deleting it and deciding that closure can sometimes be a one-way door.

It is 3:27 a.m. and I am lying down on my bed and staring at the ceiling. The branches outside are casting shadows on the walls and it looks like I live in a forest. Tears are streaming down the sides of my face. The house is quiet and calm, but I haven't slept in days. The impact of my mother's actions in my life are immeasurable and I cannot make sense of them. How could she never have explained or told anyone what happened? Why didn't she tell my brothers the version of events that I told her? What *does* my father know, if anything at all? It was clear to me that whatever Lyle did to me was never mentioned and somehow another narrative was created, downplayed, and ultimately swept under the rug. Why? Why did the people that were supposed to love me the most leave me in the trenches to deal with something that wasn't my fault? Who decided that I was the one that was to be ostracized? Who made me the scapegoat? Why was I made to believe I was defective with my 'problems' when Lyle was the one that abused me? How could my mother let this happen? How could my mother permit my victimization this way for so long when she knew I was damaged because of the abuse? I did not know how or who was going to answer these questions or how I was going to stop these thoughts thrashing in my head.

Does anyone realize at all what was taken away from

me? How I could have had a different relationship with my father and brothers or how it could have been different each time someone hugged me so that I felt comfort instead of repulsion? Doesn't anyone understand how important it is to feel loved? And all of this because someone violated me, and I screamed for help. Why was *I* being punished for Lyle's sins?

I am still in a daze a few days later when the phone rings and the caller ID reads *Joseph*.

"Yep," I respond. We hadn't spoken much as I was avoiding contact with my family.

"I called Mom, Dad and Philip earlier this morning. We are meeting at Mom and Dad's at noon. Bring the letter to read to Dad."

"Okay," I respond apathetically without protest. I know I will not win when he is this determined, and I know that my life has changed again. I was not sure I was ready for another round of the 'sex abuse scandal' discussion with my mother, but I needed to understand and get clarification on what role my mother played.

TEN

COLLATERAL DAMAGE

A few hours later I am sitting in front of my father. My mother is to my right and my brothers are standing up. My mother is smiling but not understanding why we are all gathered. I am raging inside. I don't want to accept what the truth might be and what I think it is. Before reading the letter I apologize to my father.

"For what?" he asks.

"For what I'm about to tell you and for what you are about to know. I'm sorry it's going to hurt you. I love you," I tell him. He looks back at me confused. I look down and begin reading the letter out loud. Despite being a full-grown adult, I feel shameful and embarrassed to read some parts in front of my brothers and father. At the end, my father burst into tears. "I didn't know this happened to you," he said. "I had no idea this is what happened." I hug my father and comfort him telling him it's okay. As I do, I hear my mother's voice in my ears say "Me neither. I never heard all of these things." The world suddenly stops spinning and I am frozen.

"What?" I ask turning to her. "What did you just say?" Everyone turns to look at my mother.

"That I never knew. That you never told me these things." I stare at her mouth while the words are coming out and want to explode. Instead, I hold my temper being mindful that we are not alone, and my father just found out his daughter was sexually abused.

"Don't tell me you didn't know. How dare you tell me you didn't know? I told you what he did. How do you not remember? I ran away from home because of it," I said.

"Yes you told me he touched you," she begins to say and then I interrupt her, "THE LIVING ROOM MOM, don't you remember? Don't you remember what I told you in the living room? And then you sent me to the doctor the next day?"

"Yes," she confirms.

"Did you know he did those things?" Philip asked.

"Yes," my mother responded. "But not in this way."

"So instead of saying I didn't tell you, do me a favor and say you don't remember because I told you Mom. We talked about this more than once over the years." I am livid, and I can barely stand to look at her.

"You didn't know?" I turn asking my father. "No," he replies tearfully. "I was under the impression that he walked by you and touched your chest by mistake. If I had known this is what happened I would have reacted and done things differently. I'm so sorry. Please forgive me." As I listen to my father's tearful apology for something that he didn't do, the rage I have towards my mother is blinding. I cannot believe she did not tell my father. My heart breaks for him. I spent my entire life cringing at the thought of being in the same room as him or, even worse, receiving a hug from him. The anger that I had towards my father because I thought he knew of the abuse tainted every single interaction I had with him. I look down at his hands, full of wrinkles and creases and try to hold back from breaking down.

"Please don't apologize, Dad. There is nothing you need to apologize for. You didn't know. How can I blame you for acting the way you did if you didn't know?" I turn to my brothers. Joseph looks at me apologetically and says, "We knew what Dad knew and we were told not to react and that it wasn't a big deal. We did what we were told and I'm sorry that we did."

Everyone is upset and my brothers continue to hammer my mother with questions. "Why didn't you tell us the real story? Do you realize he should have gone to jail for the things he did to Rosemary? Our whole life we wondered about this, and you didn't tell us what really happened or even what you knew.'

I sit back and listen to the conversation, but my mind wanders and wonders what else could have been different in my life if the situation was dealt with differently. I tune out completely until I leave to go home. It hurts too much to think. It hurts too much to feel. I am unable to wrap my head around the situation and drive in silence, taking the long way home so that I can pull over and cry easily if needed.

I take my time going home using the backroads to arrive trying to avoid busy streets. I can't stop crying. I am not sobbing, I can see clearly in front of me, and I am calm, but the tears keep falling from my eyes. *What can my mother possibly mean that it is the first time she heard it like that?*

She was there for all of it and knew, detail by detail, about the first time he touched me. She knew about his comments...she knew, she knew, she knew, she knew, she knew, she knew, I kept repeating in my head. I felt as though I was short circuiting. *I can't believe she told me she didn't know. She knew. She knew he sexually abused me.*

I was broken. I felt as though there had been a cut in the fabric of my life. Once again, there was a 'before' and an 'after'. I always had a feeling that no one in my family knew he sexually abused me, but I was reassured by my mother that yes, everyone was well aware of what he had done to me. *I was right. I wasn't imagining things. I felt that no one knew what he did, and I was right.* The validation I felt in the emotional absorption of that information was the buoy that kept me afloat. Slowly, I began to unravel the truth and saw with a new light, a different life appear before my eyes. It was all over. Everything suddenly and immediately felt lighter. *There was nothing wrong with me!* I smiled through my tears feeling as though I had just taken Red Pill. It was over. The weight had been lifted. I did not know how I was ever going to speak to my mother again, however, I felt I had overcome at least one gigantic emotional hurdle.

After uncovering that my mother was not truthful and that she too tried to sweep the abuse under the rug I did not contact her for a long while. I spent six months coming to terms with what she failed to do for me, and then ultimately decided I would not let her mistakes affect my life or relationships anymore. I wanted to be close to my family and knew the only way this would happen would be if I accepted her back into my life. Initially I created boundaries but little by little my mother began to comprehend how the impact of her actions altered the course of my life. I sat down and explained to her with a lot of patience, what my day-to-day life was like because of the impact of the abuse. Over time my mother connected it all and also comprehended that my struggles had everything to do with how the abuse was handled since the abuse shaped how I viewed the world, and in turn, the choices I made. My mother saw those things, and in seeing and recognizing them, I was healing a little each day.

"The problem with all of this is that our lives are so intertwined. Where does that leave our family? Are your brothers going to follow suit to support you? How does this affect future family visits to Canada? Is everyone going to skip going to Canada, Florida or Italy to avoid the awkwardness? Or will my kids not know your family anymore? Lastly, how much power are you going to give Lyle over our lives?"

I reread Regina's text and shake my head. It sends chills down my spine remembering how heavy my life felt before I took it back. Before the letter to her sister and before I stopped lying to everyone including myself. The text enraged me at first, but after a while it just made me sad for her. Whoever I thought Regina was and the person I admired so much growing up only existed in my mind. If she believed exposing her brother-in-law made him more powerful, I wanted nothing to do with her twisted mentality. Her words were a feeble, desperate attempt at keeping the status quo and I wasn't interested.

It is a week before I was leaving for the beach house and my mother calls from Italy asking me if I have a minute. Her face looks worried, and I ask her what's wrong.

"They are coming," she says to me.

"What?" I respond knowing exactly what she means. "All of them?" I ask.

"Yes," she responds and shakes her head. We look at each other without saying a word. I know it is not her fault and she is just telling me what she knows. My heart sinks. I was really excited about the trip but there would be no way I'd be going now.

"Ok," I respond shaking my head. I end the call and begin searching my emails for the flight booking. I begin to feel dizzy but keep searching. There is no way I was going to the beach house with Lyle there. And why didn't Tamara find out if I was going to be there or not? Wasn't that the 'deal?' The anger I feel instantly raises my blood pressure. *Does she actually think that even after all this time I want to see him? Why would I want that? What kind of a sick mind would think that I would want him near me?* The complete and utter dismissal of my feelings hits me like a brick. My stomach begins to turn, and my throat starts to close. *Even after I sent her that letter.* I think, *what kind of a person reads a letter like that from a family member and decides to go back on an agreement made long ago? Even as a fellow woman. Why would she do that to another woman?* I am repulsed and nauseous by the thought of her.

I take a few deep breaths and decide to go for a walk to clear my mind. I hike fifteen kilometers before turning around to walk back home to ask my parents if they knew of anyone that would rent me an apartment close by.

A few days later my mother calls and I accept her video call request. I see she's not at home. I am in the process of packing my bags to leave since another family member so graciously offered their home to me for the time I was there.

"Hello?" I respond.

"I did it!" my mother whispers urgently. My mother's face is blurred, and I see her hair blowing in the wind. *Is she at the beach?* I wonder.

"What did you do?"

"I told them," she continues in the same whisper aiming her mouth towards the speaker of the phone, "I told them to leave me alone because their father is a pedophile and he molested you when you were young."

I can't believe what I'm hearing. I ask her to clarify what had happened and she tells me that she was on the beach and approached by Jessica. She asked Jessica to please keep away from her as she wanted nothing to do with her or her family since Lyle molested me when I was young. The wind keeps picking up, and my mother does not want to speak in public, so she tells me she'll call me later. I hang up the phone in shock. *What just happened?* I thought. *Did I just hear correctly?* I begin to laugh but realize I'm also crying. With each chuckle and tear I feel my shoulders becoming lighter. *Did she actually use the word pedophile when referring to Lyle?* I sit down on my bed and wait for my mother's call back.

We speak face-to-face online a short time later when she returns from the beach, and I listen intently as though afraid my ears may suddenly stop working. I listen to every detail and watch her mouth moves as she speaks. She repeats what she started to tell me at the beach and finishes the story with how she told both Jessica and Simon, in two different short conversations, that she understood they had nothing to do with it, but she could not associate with them anymore since their father is a pedophile and molested me when I was young. I ask her if anyone heard her.

"I really don't think so. I said it in English and spoke directly to each of them," she responded, "I didn't want to say a thing, but I felt forced. I felt like I could not hold it in anymore. Of course, I didn't want to do it in that way. I didn't even plan it to be honest but how on earth was I expected to socialize with them or be civil with him around? I know I did not speak loudly, I made sure of it. After a few minutes they left the beach and went back to the house. I'm not sure if they are downstairs or not but I don't care. I'm fine in my home with my apartment door closed and locked."

As I look at her I watch her lips move and hear her words, but I cannot believe it is my mother. I had never seen her so comfortable in her own skin. She was confident and spoke with conviction. "I asked my sister Giulia if she could find ways to keep them as far from me as possible. She knows where I settle in at the beach every day. Could she not have redirected them and gone somewhere else? She argued with me and called it ridiculous that the issue was being brought up again after all these years." I chuckled thinking of what those years looked like for me. I guess some people don't see the prisons of others.

"Do you think Jessica and Simon knew?" I ask.

"I don't know. If Tamara didn't tell them then they would have been shocked but then again, if Lyle had kept his hands to himself, none of this would have happened. We asked Tamara to keep him away from our family if she chose to stay with him, and for a few years it worked."

"Yes, I remember," I say recalling all of the times arrangements were made by Tamara and other family members to ensure Lyle and I would not run into each other.

"Over time," my mother continued, "She chose to ignore the agreement we made and slowly pushed him back into our lives. I don't understand why she chose to stay with him but that's not my problem and none of my business. I still can't believe that the first time he touched you he was thirty-four years old, and you were twelve."

"I know. It's surreal to think that today I am forty-seven years old. It's been over thirty years that I have been living with this hate for myself, yet all of the bad feelings have nothing to do with me. I did nothing wrong. It feels so good to know that but more importantly feel that."

"Why? What did you do wrong? You were twelve years old. Why would you ever feel like you did something wrong?" My mother asked.

"I know you are right and in a logical world I see your point. Internally, I did not feel that way. My reaction was that I froze every time Lyle did something. Somehow I felt that by my body doing that meant I enabled it somehow. Now I understand that freezing is my survival response so in actuality, the reason I was freezing was because I was actively being traumatized. Obviously, I didn't see it that way. There are a lot of things that get jumbled up in your head when something like this happens to you. Going to the beach house for example is something I love and hate at the same time. I love to go because it is like another home for me, but I hate to go since I deal with more flashbacks and nightmares while I'm there. To me, my whole life I felt as though I was being constantly visited by ghosts."

"What do you mean ghosts?" my mother asked.

"Something that reminds me of him or the abuse some-how. Like when someone puts a hand on the middle of my back. I feel his hand on my back. I could not hug people for years because I felt his hands all over me, all over again. It's hard receiving affection and comfort and I have to work through it."

"Does this happen even now?" my mom asks.

"Sometimes it does but I can shake it off quickly."

"How do you feel now?" my mother asks.

"I feel good. I'm glad it's out in the open this way. I can't believe you did that," I say to my mother knowing full well that words would not be able to express the catharsis that her action initiated. I was still in shock that she had done something so bold and could not find a way to express the impact of what she did.

"I should have done it long ago," my mother comments. "I feel better too now as I didn't realize how much this has weighed on me."

"I know it did," I respond reassuring my mother. "I know this was a nightmare for you as well." I end the call with my mother and sit back on the chair closing my eyes.

I felt revitalized and somehow reborn again. Within seventy-two hours of the conversation with my mother my blood pressure dropped to a range I hadn't achieved since I was eighteen years old, and my senses felt somehow like they had come out of hibernation. Food hadn't tasted so good and smells were much richer and more complex. I noticed I didn't need to concentrate on my breathing as much to keep my voice steady and my world appeared more vibrant in my eyes. Colours seemed more colourful some-how. My breathing was not irregular, and my body felt younger. Physically, I felt as though my body had gone back in time. I was amazed at the way my body felt and the way I physically felt changed after my mother validated the abuse in the manner she did. Something changed in me, I felt it but could not put it into words. I felt like my mother saw me for the first time as the person I was instead of the person that I pretended to be. She saw me as her daughter that was sexually abused and manipulated to stifle it.

It was as though a blanket of acceptance and love was placed around my shoulders and I began to walk towards myself again, finally feeling whole and present in body and mind.

EPILOGUE

I named it. I named him. I named what he did to me. I named what it felt like, and I named the effects it had on me. And if I can name it all, I know I am not alone. If you are reading this. Neither are you. Wherever I go I never forget:

- No one is coming to change or save your life. It's yours. Do the best you can with the opportunities, choices and chances in front of you. Play the cards you have been dealt.
- Accept yourself, trust yourself, validate yourself, embrace yourself, love yourself, even when no one else does. No one has the ability to step into your consciousness and experience your world and until this can happen, no one can judge your actions or decisions you've made.
- Accept your hardships by looking at them differently. Contrary to popular belief,

hardships can be gifts. There are lessons to be learned with each gift and ignoring what is uncomfortable will only limit you to seeing and using only a part of the gift you've been given.

- Accept what happened to you and accept what is happening to you. Take care of your body. Trauma does not make you stronger, it causes chaos to your nervous system, changes your brain function, burns a hole in your stomach, keeps your body hypervigilant, isolates you and does its best to kill you in one way or another. Be kind to yourself. Be compassionate. Your body is your home. Be the person you needed to protect and nurture you. Do not underestimate the effect of emotional stress on the body. It can surprise you.

- Learn how to breathe through pain, it is your best weapon when your nervous system works against you.

- Do the right thing, even if no one is watching or asking.

- Be compassionate and have empathy. Understand that as your experiences have shaped you, other people have been shaped by their own experiences.

- It only takes thirty seconds of raw courage to do the thing you think you cannot do. All will fall into place eventually; your job is to make sure you keep moving towards your goal.

- People are found in what they do; when someone shows you who they are, believe them.

- If you are accused of something you didn't do, be sure it is something your accuser has done, would do or is thinking of doing. Remember that projection is sometimes the only confession you will ever receive.

- You do not need anyone else to feel closure. You can do it all by yourself by recognizing and accepting the way you were or are treated is unacceptable. Closure can be a door that you close, you don't need the other person to see it or acknowledge it.
- Life is in a constant state of flux. You have already survived what you think you could not.
- You belong to yourself. Do not change for anyone.
- Your greatest weaknesses are your greatest strengths cloaked in fear.

ACKNOWLEDGMENTS

Thank you to Perry Power, Emma Mack, Sonia Guzman and the entire Powerful Books Community for your unwavering and unconditional love, patience, and encouragement throughout the writing process.

Perry, you were the hand that reached for me in the dark and I could never express into words how grateful I am to you for this. I took your hand blindly, an ocean away, and you never let go. I will never forget how you changed my life and helped me see who I was and how powerful I can be.

Emma, your resilience is legendary and you have a special place in my heart as the person who taught me the most about acceptance, and choice.

Sonia, my accountability partner and my sister that helped me stay *"sunny as fuck"* and on track. I'm never letting you go so get used to me.

Thank you to Amanda for helping me untangle my thoughts week after week, year after year. The dedication and care I receive from you does not go unnoticed. Your pearls of wisdom and the lessons I have learned from you and our talks have been instrumental in helping me move forward and live more authentically.

Thank you to my family of friends including, but not limited to, Lori Gibbons, Andrea Macari, Tammy Johnson, Laura Gennaro, Graziano Roti, Steve Buttigieg and Jenni

Hill. As Bradley Cooper says in Silver Linings Playbook, "I got nothing but love for you, brother".

Thank you to my father and brothers; you have been pillars of support for me, holding me up in different ways throughout my life. I love you deeply and appreciate you immensely.

Grazie mamma, how do I thank you? You have given me the chance to experience two completely different lives. Despite what you may feel, I am incredibly grateful for both of them and for each and every lesson I learned to bring me where I am today, in this imperfect, exquisite world.

To you, a te, you know who you are. I love you immensely. Thank you for being you and accepting me for me. You are the best thing I ever found at the mall.

Printed in the USA
CPSIA information can be obtained
at www.ICGtesting.com
LVHW092201210224
772507LV00005B/170